Goodbye, YESTERDAY!

Goodbye,
YESTERDAY!

CINDY TRIMM

🔥 CHARISMA HOUSE

GOODBYE, YESTERDAY! by Cindy Trimm
Published by Charisma House
Charisma Media/Charisma House Book Group
600 Rinehart Road, Lake Mary, Florida 32746

Library of Congress Cataloging-in-Publication Data:
An application to register this book for cataloging has been submitted to the Library of Congress.
International Standard Book Number: 978-1-62999-623-3
E-book ISBN: 978-1-62999-624-0

20 21 22 23 24 — 987654321
Printed in the United States of America

CONTENTS

◆ ◆ ◆

INTRODUCTION

◆ ◆ ◆

*We are all at the center of our
own narrative, but it's a narrative that
changes every time we retell it.*
—Ruth Ware

THERE IS SOMETHING that all of us can learn from our life experiences once we interpret them through the lens of faith. Some lessons are painful, and some are painless, but none of them are pointless. The first chapter of the Book of Genesis is brilliantly written to help us retell our stories so that we can reframe our lives.

The stories we tell ourselves about our past experiences determine our future. According to a recent *Forbes* article, "The single biggest predictor for all these [life] events is not the facts of your situation, but the story you tell."[1] The article went on to explain that there is an epidemic of negative storytelling in our culture that is pervading our personal and interior lives. That sounds grim. But the article's writer adds that "the good news is that we have the ability to fix that. And the best news is that it's not as hard as you might believe."[2]

Psychologist Kelly McGonigal has observed that "small shifts in mindset can trigger a cascade of changes so profound that they test the limits of what seems possible."[3] When you truly believe "all things work together for good to them that love God" (Rom. 8:28), your perspective will change, and in retrospect you will see God bringing you through the most difficult of times—and you will realize that not one moment of your life is wasted.

What are the words you use to tell your story?

To reset and reclaim your life, you will have to reframe the narrative of your life story so that it mirrors the narrative God originally planned and purposed. If you want to leave behind the baggage that is weighing you down, you'll have to learn to tell your story from a different vantage point—the vantage point of faith. The stories you choose to tell today—whether woven in faith or fear; resentment, regret, or gratitude—shape the tomorrows of your future. The story God chose to tell in the first chapter of Genesis shaped the world as we know it today. I chose to weave the story of Genesis into the message of this book because it will help you understand how to shape your everyday life. This book is written to help you achieve perspective and gain a greater appreciation for the God who lives inside of you. He is your "refuge and strength, a very present help in trouble" (Ps. 46:1).

In the first installment of this three-book series, *Commanding Your Morning*, you learned the importance of watching your words. So many people walk around with their lives on stutter and auto-repeat because they keep telling the same stories about their past over and over again. In the second installment, *Hello, Tomorrow!*, you learned how forming a vision for your life can help you break negative cycles because your tomorrow does not have to look like your yesterday. In this final installment, *Goodbye, Yesterday!*, you will learn that all of us have potential for greatness—for accomplishing great things, establishing amazing relationships, and creating astounding masterpieces of our lives. Potential is God's gift to you. Maximizing your potential is your gift to Him.

After a great deal of prayer and meditation on how to share a fresh message of faith with the many books already written, I discovered beautiful truths from the creation story, found in Genesis. From the very first chapter of Genesis, I extrapolated principles I felt could help you get unstuck and break free from the negative cycles holding sway over your life and potentially over your family and community. I saw concepts and keys that would enable you to quit repeating the same old cycles over and over again by reframing your past, recharging your present, reclaiming your future, and restoring your destiny.

While we intuitively understand that the past shapes the future, the present also shapes how we see the past. You can recalibrate your present reality not only by creating a new vision of the future[4] but also by recreating the vision you hold of your past experiences. I realize you can never go back to your past to begin again, but you can start now to script a new future by telling a new story. You will be able to stand in agreement with God's word for your life so that, unfettered by your past, you will be able to declare with boldness, "I come in the volume of the book that is written of me!" (See Psalm 40:7.)

THE FORCE OF FAITH

The Scripture says, "Through faith we understand the worlds were framed by the word of God" (Heb. 11:3). So how are you, who were made in His image, framing your own life? Often we frame our lives based on past failures or disappointments. We go from person to person, relationship to relationship, telling our sad stories, wondering why nothing ever seems to improve. We must learn to change the narrative, to reframe the past so that by faith we might frame a better future for ourselves and those we love.

The insights from Genesis presented in this book will help you create a new story for your life and bolster your faith. The story of Genesis is not just about beginnings; it is about new beginnings. Here we are introduced to how God reframed His reality and how we are able to reframe ours. Where did God start in the fashioning and reforming of an earth that was laid waste? He didn't become a commentator or complainer of chaos and darkness; instead, in His omnipotence He spoke light.

So it should be with you and me. We must start exactly where we are right now. We must ask God to bring enlightenment to our minds and give us wisdom so that we may make decisions that would bring our lives into alignment with His will. You cannot start where you are not. You can only start from where you are. From this point on, you must take 100 percent responsibility for your life. You must resist blaming others. Lean less on others and more on God. Even as God fully embraced His creative ability to reframe, recreate, recharge, and restore the atmosphere the way He desired it to be, so can you. He did not call those things that were as if they were not. He did not wish things would change and complacently wait. No! He engaged the power of the spoken word and called those things that were not as though they were (Rom. 4:17).

He demonstrated for us how faith fuels our future. Faith starts with positivity and being able to decide what we are going to do with where we are. Faith is like a GPS system; it doesn't start where you want to end up. Instead, it starts where you are, and that's exactly where you need to be to start. Wishing you were someplace else is not the same as being someplace else. You have to put action to your desires, dreams, and goals— because "faith without works is dead" (Jas. 2:20).

One of my mentors, Les Brown, spoke about how he had struggled with so many negative emotions about his adoption. One day a friend heard him speaking negatively about his experience and told him that he had to change the way he was thinking about this particular situation. He said to Les that while most children are born to parents who did not choose them, his adoptive mother walked into that room and chose him out of love. She wasn't forced to adopt him but instead chose to—and more importantly chose *him*. Les recounts that moment as being destiny altering. In that moment he had a change of perspective and thus a change of narrative.

Likewise, you and I have been chosen in Christ by love, and this gives us the opportunity to change our perspective about our lives and our own narratives. That choice gives us the ability to do what many other people cannot: begin again.

> Therefore if any man be in Christ, he is a new creature: old things are passed away; behold, all things are become new.
>
> —2 Corinthians 5:17

In Christ we are born again. You are an all-new creation waking up each day to God's mercies that are new every morning (Lam. 3:22–23). It's not by our might, nor by our power, but by the Spirit of the Lord (Zech. 4:6).

Les Brown had to reframe the narrative of his past. When he did, he was able to overcome the negative emotions of resentment and shame. This all happened the moment he was able to readjust his perspective and tell a new story about who he was. As a result, today he is one of the most influential and impactful motivational speakers of our generation.

You have so much potential that has been capped by the emotional lids you've nailed down within yourself, self-imposed limitations that keep you from moving ahead into your greater destiny. You were young, immature, and vulnerable when many things happened to you. But now you don't have to live your life from a place of vulnerability. You can take your personal power back!

This book is about loving yourself into the destiny you've dreamed of and the awesome future God has for you. It is about regaining perspective and reigniting faith. It's about the different dynamics of faith that will empower you to go where God has ordained you to go.

Faith is a discipline that must be exercised, and it is a law that must be executed. As you are introduced to the twelve laws of boundary-defying faith, you will learn the rules and protocols for activating them. You will be equipped to practically apply each principle to redirect your life.

It is my prayer that as you read through the four sections of this book, you will experience an incredible turnaround. I pray that you will be able to wave goodbye to yesterday as you reframe, recharge, reclaim, and restore your faith in the tomorrows of your dreams! If you have made it this far in spite of your challenges, setbacks, and sidesteps, what other awesome things are you capable of achieving? The last chapter of your life is yet to be written. Make this next chapter epic!

PART ONE

• • •

Reframe

CHAPTER 1

Put First Things First

THE LAW OF PRIORITIZATION

In the beginning God created
the heaven and the earth.
—GENESIS 1:1

ADEFENSE ATTORNEY STEPS to the front of the courtroom. A
hush falls on the people as he begins his opening argument,
his airtight defense. His statement is well prepared because it is
truth, and it will establish the facts beyond a reasonable doubt.
With unfettered confidence he opens.

> "In the beginning was the Word, and the Word was with
> God, and the Word was God....All things were made
> through Him, and without Him nothing was made that
> was made. In Him was life, and the life was the light
> of men" [JOHN 1:1, 3–4, NKJV]....He is the "Alpha and
> Omega, the first and the last" [REVELATION 1:11]. We
> need look no further for "the author and finisher of our
> faith" [HEBREWS 12:2]. I have no further remarks.

Who is this God who was there in the beginning? Nothing is revealed to us about the background or qualifications of the mastermind Creator God. We are simply introduced to the divine engineer, God Himself, who alone can speak on His behalf. Therefore, let the record show His stated introduction: "I AM THAT I AM" (Exod. 3:14).

By His own word He made the following statement, as the prophet Isaiah recorded verbatim:

> I am the First and I am the Last; besides Me there is no God. And who can proclaim as I do? Then let him declare it and set it in order for Me, since I appointed the ancient people. And the things that are coming and shall come, let them show these to them. Do not fear, nor be afraid; have I not told you from that time, and declared it? You are My witnesses. Is there a God besides Me? Indeed there is no other Rock; I know not one.
>
> —ISAIAH 44:6–8, NKJV

The opening statement of Genesis 1:1 does not talk of God's ancestry, for it is accepted that He always was and will always be the self-existing eternal One—the "LORD God Almighty, which was, and is, and is to come" (Rev. 4:8). No formal curriculum vitae is needed to qualify Him. Nothing is added to satiate our curiosity, confirm our theology, ratify our philosophy, or validate our hypothesis. This opening sentence is presented as an incontestable statement of fact and therefore is expected to be received with unquestioning faith, for it is "through faith we understand that the worlds were framed by the word of God, so that things which are seen were not made of things which do appear" (Heb. 11:3).

God's opening arguments describing His creative activity, which the entire body of Scripture corroborates and which historical evidence has done more to validate than disprove, defy any notion of atheistic unbelief. The universe was brought into existence by the creative God, not through any natural process. Non-Christian philosopher J. S. Mill declared, "For nature to make itself is a scientific impossibility."[1] Author Fritz Chery writes, "Atheism can't explain existence. Atheists live by science, but science (always) changes. God and the Bible (always) remain the same."[2]

How did God create the universe? He created it through the supernatural energy of faith. God's words revealed His faith, which is "the substance of things hoped for" (Heb. 11:1). What He hoped for became substance, our universe.

BEGINNING AGAIN IS AN ONGOING PROCESS

In the epic opening verse of the Bible, two key words help us understand its deeper meaning. The word *beginning* is from the Hebrew *re'shiyth*,[3] which does not include the article *the* and could perhaps more accurately be translated "at *a* beginning." What does this mean for us? God is the God of new beginnings, of continual renewal, of new mercies every morning (Lam. 3:22–23).

Life is full of fresh starts. Every new beginning requires a decision. God made a decision at the time of the beginning when He set in motion the creation of the heavens and the earth. Any new beginning is a choice. You choose at the dawn of each new day to get out of bed. You choose to trust that God will be with you all day. You choose whether to pray. You choose the thoughts you think and the words you speak. You choose both what goes in your mouth and what comes out of it. You always have a choice.

Don't ever think you are without options or that your situation defies solving. As long as you choose to allow the Spirit of God to work in your life, you will always have an opportunity to choose a different outcome. Even if the only choice you make today is to honor God by putting your faith in Him and maintaining a positive attitude in the face of the negativity around you, your choice will change the atmosphere. Your Holy Spirit–infused energy will affect the environment to such a degree that eventually things will turn in your favor.[4]

Sow in gratitude, and reap in favor. There is no other way to enter God's presence, to enter His courts, than through thanksgiving and praise (Ps. 100:4). The antidote for an undertow of bitterness is waves of gratitude. So many people are bitter, which is the fruit of self-pity. But when you take your mind off yourself and your circumstances and set your thoughts on your heavenly Father and His kingdom, your bitterness will take flight.

You don't have to live in fear when faith is made available to you on demand. As Jesus repeatedly instructs, "Fear not: believe only" (Luke 8:50). When you experience a detrimental setback, faith allows you to know that God is working on a supernatural setup! The same God who, through the quickening power of the Holy Spirit, brought forth life on the land and beneath the sea in Genesis 1 will bring forth amazing things in your life. He will quicken the potential and the dormant gifts He placed in you before you were born.

"Choose this day whom you will serve" (Josh. 24:15, ESV). Choose to change your future by activating your faith, not only in God, but in the person He created you to be. Remember, what lies ahead of you is far greater than what lies behind you. And what lies inside of you is far greater than them both. God is always in the process of maturing you, of building your capacity to become and achieve more, of maximizing the potential He placed in you the day you were conceived. See yourself as God sees you. Lean on Him. Rely on Him. Learn to trust and delight in Him; "lean not on your own understanding" (Prov. 3:5). You must simply choose a new beginning, a fresh start.

One of the best times to make a new beginning is when something comes to an end. Novelist Arnold Bennett once said, "The chief beauty about the constant supply of time is that you cannot waste it in advance. The next year, the next day, the next hour are lying ready for you, as perfect, as unspoilt, as if you had never wasted or misapplied a single moment in all your career.... You can turn over a new leaf every hour if you choose."[5]

Couple these thoughts with what you can learn from the word *create* from Genesis 1:1. It is from the Hebrew *bara'*, which indeed means "to form" or "to create" but also has the connotation of cutting down or cutting out.[6] Just as some believe that sculpting is a process of cutting away the superfluous to reveal the figure inside the marble, God is always in the process of cutting away the superfluous from your life.

Throughout the Bible flows the idea of removing things that are detrimental to you. "Get rid of all bitterness, rage, anger, harsh words, and slander" (Eph. 4:31, NLT). "Get rid of all moral filth and the evil that is so prevalent" (Jas. 1:21, NIV). Get rid of "all the historical and religious junk so that the unshakable essentials stand clear and uncluttered" (Heb. 12:27, MSG).

This culling is as much a process of beginning as it is of creating. You can't create the new without shedding the old. For "no one puts new wine into old wineskins. For the wine would burst the wineskins, and the wine and the skins would both be lost. New wine calls for new wineskins" (Mark 2:22, NLT). What are some old wineskins you need to get rid of? What are some old things to which you need to say goodbye so you can say hello to something new?

My personal and professional experiences have shown me this isn't as easy to do as it sounds. If it were, I wouldn't need to write an entire book about it. But the simple truths found in God's Word represent spiritual laws you can choose to activate in your life. These clear principles and practical strategies will help you say goodbye to whatever is holding you back from your preferred tomorrow. For we know as fact that God has given you all you need for life and godliness (2 Pet. 1:3). He has given you the power and potential to create the life of your dreams. In fact it is God who has given you the power to dream. You are made in His Creator image; you have the DNA of the ultimate imagineer. If God can reimagine a new day with the dawn of each new morning, He can help you reimagine your life.

God is in the business of creating something out of nothing, of finding that beautiful sculpture hidden in the rock. He wants to cut out all that is superfluous. All He requires is that you let go of some things, disentangle yourself from emotional soul ties,[7] and get rid of the clutter and minutiae that keep you from entering His rest, that junk in your trunk that stiffens your neck and hardens your heart. Don't fall short of entering the rest He has prepared for you.

> Since it still remains for some to enter that rest, and since those who formerly had the good news proclaimed to them did not go in because of their disobedience, God again set a certain day, calling it "Today."..."Today, if you hear His voice, do not harden your hearts."
>
> —HEBREWS 4:6–7, NIV

As a born-again citizen of the kingdom of heaven, you are invited into God's perfect peace and protected place of divine prosperity.[8] Let God show you what you need to leave behind so He can bring you into the promises He has prepared for you. This is a journey of faith. It takes faith to let go and let God move in your circumstances. It takes faith to believe He is working all things together for your greatest good (Rom. 8:28). It takes faith to trust that God has your best interest at heart, that He not only loves you but also cares for you (1 Pet. 5:7). He watches over you (Ps. 121) and will establish you (1 Pet. 5:10). It takes faith to trust that He is faithful (1 Cor. 10:13). That simple faith requires you to keep your eyes on Him (Heb. 12:2) and on His goodness and grace.

The Bible starts with God, and all things good emanate from there. "God saw all that he had made, and it was very good" (Gen. 1:31, NIV) because "everything good comes from God" (Jas. 1:17, ERV). That's why I believe whoever starts with God will also come into all things good.

THE LAW OF PRIORITIZATION

Some things seem too simple to be true, such as the truth that when you put God first, He will take care of the rest. "For your heavenly Father knows that you need all these things. But seek first the kingdom of God and His righteousness, and all these things shall be added to you" (Matt. 6:32–33, NKJV). That is not very complicated, is it? Wisdom 101 would say, "Trust in the LORD with all your heart, and lean not on your own understanding; in all your ways acknowledge Him, and He shall direct your paths" (Prov. 3:5–6, NKJV).

The one thing above everything else you are called to do is simply "love the LORD your God with all your heart, with all your soul, with all your mind, and with all your strength. This is the first commandment" (Mark 12:30, NKJV). Why is this so critical to your moving beyond your past and into the future you've envisioned?[9] Because this one discipline concerns how you choose to posture your heart, which will enable you to focus on what is important and to prioritize what is required.

If you read through the Bible, you will see the overarching theme of God's great love for you. The good thing is, God is unchangeable, so you can have confidence in His love for you. God is for you, and He is cheering you on. "If God is for us, who can be against us? He who did not spare His own Son, but delivered Him up for us all, how shall He not with Him also freely give us all things?" (Rom. 8:31–32, NKJV).

Make God your priority in all things. Make your relationship with Him more important than anything else. Love is an act of intimacy. It is a gift from God and is the precursor to faith. Just as love is a gift, so is faith.

Faith is trusting in the all-sufficiency of your God, whose love leads you beyond just trusting Him to letting Him heal you. Faith is trusting the healer Himself. It is not just trusting God to supply all your needs but trusting Jehovah Jireh Himself. It is not about the gift but the giver of the gift.

It is not easy to trust God for His provision, protections, and prosperity, especially in the midst of trying times and challenging circumstances. Faith is risky business because we want predictability. Over time we learned to do things our own way, in our own strength. We learned to be self-sufficient. But making God, His kingdom, and His righteousness priorities will enable you to align your faith, motivations, decisions, and actions to be positioned for success.

With God as your priority, you will be able to structure the routines of your life, the thoughts of your mind, and all your objectives and behaviors wisely. God will work in you "to will and to do for His good pleasure" (Phil. 2:13, NKJV). You will recognize His voice and discern His will in every situation. You will be so focused on running the race set before you, pressing "toward the goal for the prize of the upward call of God" (Phil. 3:14, NKJV), that you will forget the regrets or heartaches that have kept you down in the past. This "one thing I do," wrote Paul, "forgetting those things which are behind and reaching forward to those things which are ahead" (v. 13, NKJV). Stop letting the memory of a bad yesterday ruin a potentially good today or sabotage an awesome tomorrow. We are promised in Isaiah that when we focus on that upward call of God—His righteousness and peace and the joy found in His presence—we will have His peace: "You will keep in perfect peace those whose minds are steadfast, because they trust in you" (Isa. 26:3, NIV).

Computers can get bogged down because too many applications are running in the background. Has that ever happened to you? So many windows and tabs are open that all you see is that spinning beach ball. How much time have you wasted watching that beach ball, waiting for an issue to be resolved? Sometimes all you can do is force quit to reboot the system.

If you're like me, you open tabs on your browser that you don't have time to look at. But you keep them open just in case, and then you forget all about them while you continue to open more tabs! It's a discipline to only keep open what you need, just the one thing that will serve your highest purpose. Likewise, when it comes to your life, it might be wise to shut down everything that's competing for your mental energy and draining your power. Some "applications" that you may have forgotten about you might need to force quit.

The law of priorities is a game-changing principle. Do not engage in any activity that does not start with God. Consult God before you form relationships, engage in activities, start a business, or contemplate a ministry. Seek God's face. Seek God first, and trust Him in the process. Don't start something and then work your way up to God. Start with God and work your way down.

> Take delight in the LORD, and he will give you your
> heart's desires. Commit everything you do to the LORD.
> Trust him, and he will help you. He will make your
> innocence radiate like the dawn, and the justice of your
> cause will shine like the noonday sun.
>
> —PSALM 37:4–6, NLT

We see this principle at work in the life of young King Uzziah, who was only sixteen years old when he came into power (2 Chron. 26:1). Of him the scripture states, "He sought God in the days of Zechariah, who had understanding in the visions of God: and as long as he sought the LORD, God made him to prosper" (v. 5). He was inspired by God to do great exploits in his day, and so you should be.

YOU GOT THIS BECAUSE GOD'S GOT YOU

What God created at the beginning was a reflection of the nature and perfection of our Creator God. His creation was worthy of His undivided attention, and that means you! Now, you can make what you want out of what God created. You are here on the earth to take dominion over His creation (Gen. 1:26). This requires faith in your Father, the Creator God. He put you in charge of your environment and gave you the mandate to take dominion over it as His designated steward. You have His seal of approval. Don't look to man, but instead, look to God to validate you. (See Luke 14:10.)

Your faith does not need to rest on the culture's wisdom or today's science. Instead, it rests on the Word of God. "In the beginning God created" tells us that God was there at our beginning as the omnipresent eternal One, yet as a deeply personal being. You do not serve an impersonal God. You serve a God who is touchable and reachable and is "touched with the feeling of our infirmities" (Heb. 4:15). That makes Him not only the God of beginnings but also the God of new beginnings.

No matter where you find yourself in life or how far you have drifted away from Him, He can help you begin again. Just extend your faith and believe He is who He says He is. To return to God, you "must believe that he is, and that he is a rewarder of them that diligently seek him" (Heb. 11:6). We must have faith in His being, for "without faith it is impossible to please him" (v. 6). In order to do any of this, we must be able to take Him at His Word.

Every day, you have choices to make. You can choose to believe the irrefutable Word of God and be steadfast in that, or you can choose to allow outside forces to control how you respond to the circumstances of life. Trust God and make pursuing His kingdom your priority.[10] Choose to let go of the clutter of the past, and instead allow the Holy Spirit to bring the best out of your present potential. The choice belongs to no one else but you. Remember, you cannot start from where you are not but only from where you are. Where you are right now is exactly where you need to be to make a fresh start.

> From your modest beginnings, the future will be bright before you.
>
> —JOB 8:7, THE VOICE

· · ·

CHAPTER 2

Start Where You Are

THE LAW OF TRANSITION

And the earth was without form, and void;
and darkness was upon the face of the
deep. And the Spirit of God moved upon
the face of the waters. And God said, Let
there be light: and there was light. And
God saw the light, that it was good.
—GENESIS 1:2–4

WHEN GOD CREATED the heaven and the earth (Gen. 1:1),
He left His signature to ensure that everyone would know
that what He created was worthy of His undivided attention.
It was a reflection of the nature and perfection of the Creator
God, vastly different from the chaos from which the world as
we know it came forth.

The fact that the Bible says "the earth was without form,
and void" implies that this was not the original state of the
earth, and therefore we must conclude something catastrophic

occurred between Genesis 1:1 and Genesis 1:2. Author Michael Jacob explains it as follows:

> Over a hundred years ago, Dr. Chalmers pointed out that the words "the earth was waste" might equally be translated "the earth became waste." Dr. I. M. Haldeman, G. H. Pember, and others showed that the Hebrew word "was" here has been translated "became" in Gen. 19:26....We see that the world in Gen. 1:1 was quite different from the world that came after Gen. 1:3. Who can measure the distance that exists between "created" and "made"? The one is a calling into being things out of nothing, the other is a working on something already there. Man can make but cannot create. God can create as well as make.[1]

God began this wonderful creation in the midst of darkness and over the void of chaos. Yet the presence of God's Spirit hovered to bring order.

This darkness and chaos came for Milton Erickson in 1919 when he was a teenager. Erickson, an influential twentieth-century psychologist, awoke one morning to discover that parts of his body were paralyzed.[2] He soon fell into a coma, waking up three days later to find his whole body paralyzed. He could not move or speak, but he could still move his eyeballs to look around.

A few years after doctors had said he would never recover, Erickson was walking. He began with disciplining his mind, and over the next few years, he was able to reignite the neural pathways that would fire the muscles he needed to move. In the process of teaching himself the motor skills he needed to walk on his own, he observed how the unconscious mind works.

Robert Greene describes this seminal moment in *The Laws of Human Nature*:

> As if momentarily forgetting his paralysis, in his mind he began to stand up, and for a brief second, he experienced the twitching of a muscle in his leg, the first time he had felt any movement in his body at all. The doctors had told his mother he would never walk again, but they had been wrong before. Based on this simple twitch, he decided to try an experiment. He would focus deeply on a particular muscle in his leg, remembering the sensation he had before his paralysis, wanting badly to move it, and imagining it functioning again. His nurse would massage that area, and slowly, with intermittent success, he would feel a twitch and then the slightest bit of movement returning to the muscle. Through this excruciatingly slow process he taught himself to stand, then take a few steps, then walk around his room, then walk outside, increasing the distances.
>
> Somehow, by drawing upon his willpower and imagination, he was able to alter his physical condition and regain complete movement. Clearly, he realized, the mind and the body operate together, in ways we are hardly aware of.[3]

Despite his personal challenges, or perhaps because of them, Erickson went on to become both a medical doctor and a psychiatrist. Erickson's story demonstrates what Scripture declares about us in Proverbs 23:7: "For as he thinks in his heart, so is he" (NKJV). Out of Erickson's dark chaos came the light of positive transformation. Moving from where you are now to where you want to be begins in the mind.

Of course, this is easier said than done, but as with all difficult things, it becomes easier with practice. No matter what darkness and chaos swirls around you, the same Spirit that "moved upon the face of the waters" resides in you. The same Spirit of Christ that was there at the beginning is here with you now.

In Him you too can speak light into your dark situation. You can speak peace into the chaos and declare God's Word and His promises right where you are. You cannot go back in time and change the events that led to your current circumstances, but you can start where you are in the present to harness the power of your faith to redefine the future. The Holy Spirit in your life is your GPS. He knows the terrain of your destiny and will lead you from where you are to incredibly blessed places in God.

THE LAW OF TRANSITION

Erickson's health and mobility had come to an end. Between this dark diagnosis and the reclaiming of movement was a transition period, and what he did during that transition time proved crucial for his future success. The actions he took during the period between desire and manifestation led to the altering of the landscape of his future.

Transitions are not always about changing your circumstances but instead about being changed by them. Your response to these transitions will make them either bearable and fruitful or unbearable and unproductive. Your mindset will determine whether your response will default to fear or to faith. Your thinking paradigm will determine your perception of your situation. Sometimes God uses your situation to help you adjust your perception and attitude in order to increase your level of self-mastery.

The big question here is, Are you open to God showing you His ultimate plan? Are you able to say with confidence, "This is just a transition, and I'm coming out of this"? We can restrict our own growth because we have a narrow view of how God is working in our lives to build our capacity and to empower us to break through self-imposed boundaries or to broaden our influence. God is in the business of expansion. (See Isaiah 54:2.) Just as He orchestrated the universe to continually expand, so He orchestrates the events of our lives to bring us expansion.

Any type of expansion requires transition. Transition gives you the opportunity to review your past and "rescript" the narrative of your future by adjusting your perception of each experience. You can't change what happened to you in the past. You cannot go back to start over. But you can restart now to have a new ending.

Allow God to give you a new strategy. You have the mind of Christ: "Let this mind be in you, which was also in Christ Jesus: Who, being in the form of God, thought it not robbery to be equal with God: But made himself of no reputation" (Phil. 2:5–7). Sometimes you have to make yourself do things you don't feel like doing or don't believe you have the mental strength to do. This will require you to renew your mind so you can expand what you believe your capabilities to be. This is how you are transformed (Rom. 12:2). I am reminded of what Holocaust survivor Viktor Frankl observed: "When we are no longer able to change a situation...we are challenged to change ourselves."[4]

Transformation is always the result of a transition. Don't be afraid of transition because it is the only course that can take you from where you are today to where you desire to be tomorrow. Look at transition as the genesis of your transformation.

Don't struggle with your past. Instead, sit with your past struggles just long enough to review specific elements that point toward the sovereignty of God and the need for change. Remember, God has a way of using all the parts of our human experience for something even greater, something we are not always able to comprehend with our limited understanding.

You must choose to exercise faith, knowing that God's Spirit is actively working in and through your life, for you "have received, not the spirit of the world, but the Spirit who is from God, that we might know the things that have been freely given to us by God" (1 Cor. 2:12, NKJV). The Holy Spirit in your life will reveal these things to you, and you can declare them over your life. They will come as sparks of revelation, but it will be up to you to take ownership of them.

OWN WHERE YOU ARE

In the same way, God can use all your chaotic experiences for good, including every dark place of uncertainty.

> We know that all things work together for good to them
> that love God, to them who are the called according to

his purpose. For whom he did foreknow, he also did predestinate to be conformed to the image of his Son, that
he might be the firstborn among many brethren.

—ROMANS 8:28–29

Here we see the genius of God in activating human transformation. God started the transformation process in the midst
of a chaotic state. He did not bemoan the obvious but instead
called "*those things* which be not as though they were" (Rom.
4:17, emphasis added). He started with what He had and where
He was; metaphorically speaking, at the ending of one season
and the beginning of another. I use the word *season* only to
help us conceptualize the ending of something. Chaos, emp-
tiness, and darkness were coming to an end when God began
creation. We are thus able to extrapolate a principle and life
lesson that something old has to end before something new
begins.

When you have come to an end of something or have lost
something, such as a marriage, an opportunity, or a job, what
you do during the in-between time holds the secret to the success of the new season. Transitions take a great deal of faith
and patience. Being sandwiched between an ending and a
beginning is an uncertain and frustrating place to live. But that
is the order of things in nature, and so it is with you.

Our human affairs align with patterns of nature: the natural order of seasons, the sun rising and setting each day, and
the transition from childhood to adulthood, the natural beginnings and endings. Yet endings make most people fearful or
even resentful because they misuse this critical break between
seasons by looking back rather than looking ahead. It takes

faith to push past the feelings of loss. You may need to mourn your losses, but eventually you have to let go of the old before you can embrace the new.

Transitions are important for overcoming the hurt associated with loss and the pain of disappointment. Let the transition time become a period of growth that separates one season from the next, like the spring that separates the darkness of winter from the brightness of summer. After being buried in the frozen winter soil, seeds spring up to remind us of the ever present force of the potential lying dormant within the seed. On the outside nothing appears to be happening, but something is happening beneath the surface. As it is with nature, so it is with us. We must all go through transitions to get from one phase, or stage, of our lives to the next.

These times of transition allow us to gain wisdom and insight from lessons learned that can propel us into new realms of power, growth, and progress. Times of transition help us break emotional connections to past events or circumstances while emotionally connecting us through faith and hope to our next phase of growth.

Wearied by the challenges that life brings, most people try to circumvent this four-season process of ending, loss, beginning, and fruitfulness. To avoid future pain, they might even try to twist this pattern around so that beginnings come first, then endings. But this only prolongs the transition period, protracts the actual time required for preparation, exacerbates the discomfort created by the need for change, and intensifies the challenges associated with making the necessary adjustments. When you view transition as an unnecessary headache, it loses its value and purpose. Understanding that God works from sundown to sunup, rather than from sunup to sundown, might shift your perspective and help you own the time of transition that feels so dark and foreboding.

Transitions are in-between times of preparation and reflection. They are times when you can look back and gain perspective and, in doing so, clarify your vision of the future. It is a time when you can let go of things, people, attitudes, behaviors, and habits that have reached their proverbial statute of limitation. Take ownership of the in-between times when you are neither here nor there. Meditate on God's promises. Strain at clarifying your vision and goals. Transition times are important because between saying goodbye and saying hello, you can decompress and exhale as you review your experiences, assess the present, and tap into your potential in preparing for the next season. During transitions you can consult God, craft your vision, and speak into the womb of your tomorrows. It is a pregnant time when you can proactively command your mornings and decree, "Hello, tomorrow!"[5]

EMBRACE THE ENDING

One of the benefits of fully embracing an ending is seeing the value inherent in your past experiences. God uses these to break up fallow ground and clear away impediments, insecurities, and immature responses that have kept you from the greater things God has prepared for you. How you speak about your pain is just as important as how you testify about your gain. To put it in the language of the apostle Paul:

> But we have this treasure in earthen vessels, that the
> excellency of the power may be of God, and not of us.
> We are troubled on every side, yet not distressed; we
> are perplexed, but not in despair; persecuted, but not
> forsaken; cast down, but not destroyed; always bearing
> about in the body the dying of the Lord Jesus, that the
> life also of Jesus might be made manifest in our body.
> For we which live are always delivered unto death for
> Jesus' sake, that the life also of Jesus might be made
> manifest in our mortal flesh.
>
> —2 CORINTHIANS 4:7–11

When it comes to your life experiences, God either orchestrates or allows. Sometimes it is hard to connect the proverbial dots in order to see how certain unpleasant or emotionally challenging phases of your life could ever move you toward a happily-ever-after ending. But they do. I am reminded of Joseph, who in connecting his own dots of destiny was able to reassure his brothers that he held no grudge against them. Instead, he bore witness to the sovereign hand of God when he declared, "You intended to harm me, but God intended it for good to accomplish what is now being done, the saving of many lives" (Gen. 50:20, NIV). By allowing the Holy Spirit to give you God's perspective of your past, you give God the opportunity to rescript your future, primarily by changing your own assessment of yourself from being a victim to a victor (Rom. 8:37–39).

You may have misunderstood a transition before because you did not have the spiritual building blocks to understand how God was hovering over you to empower you to get through your greatest moments of challenge. "For it is God who works in you both to will and to do for His good pleasure" (Phil. 2:13, NKJV). He is always there waiting to help you navigate through the mental turbulence when you give Him permission to work on your behalf. Those are faith-building moments. I know from personal experience that it takes faith to trust God during dark, challenging, and uncertain times. It is even more challenging to maintain an attitude of gratitude in the midst of these. Plus, prayer during these moments is critical. This is my personal testimony. Prayer is a game changer.

In a blog, Dr. Caroline Leaf wrote: "It has been found that 12 minutes of daily focused prayer over an 8 week period can change the brain to such an extent that it can be measured on a brain scan. This type of prayer seems to increase activity in brain areas associated with social interaction compassion and sensitivity to others. It also increases frontal lobe activity as focus and intentionality increase. As well as changing the brain, another study implies that intentional prayer can even change physical matter. Researchers found that intentional thought for 30 seconds affected laser light."[6] In her books Dr. Leaf explains that the way we think can change the physical nature of our brains.[7] Negative thoughts actually damage our brains, but prayer and meditating on Scripture can repair that damage. The Bible tells us this, but as Dr. Leaf notes, "science is now bearing this out."[8]

Endings are about tying up loose ends and saying final goodbyes. They involve resolution and closure. To feel that closure, you may need to bid a belated farewell to a season, write a thank-you letter to a person or a season in your life, or call someone to announce you are moving on. It may mean resigning from a position you have held for years or acknowledging that a relationship or an assignment has come to an end. You may need to mentally relinquish someone you left behind years ago but never released emotionally.[9]

Changing an old image of yourself or giving up a childhood dream that has outlived its relevance might be required. Perhaps it will be time to let go of a paradigm that has held your future success in witness protection. Or you may need to finally give up a cycle of addiction or a self-defeating bad habit that you have struggled with for years. Ending a cycle of addiction or replacing a bad habit requires a great deal of courage and a great deal of support from others. Find those who have your best interest at heart and the capacity to hold you accountable, and enlist their support.

Endings are complex and complicated because they usually involve other people, whether they are people whose support you need or people from whom you need to separate. You did not expect that your source of survival, strength, happiness, or sustenance would have an expiration date. However, life is a journey, and sometimes a race requires you to leave behind the baggage you no longer need. When you consciously decide to lighten your load, you will be able to travel from one stage of development to another much more easily. Consider this beautiful invitation from your Lord and Savior:

> Come to me, all you who are weary and burdened, and I will give you rest. Take my yoke upon you and learn from me, for I am gentle and humble in heart, and you

will find rest for your souls. For my yoke is easy and my
burden is light.

—Matthew 11:28–30, niv

You can make good progress letting go of the past once you
are able to embrace grief as part of the transition process. Jesus
said, "Blessed are those who mourn, for they will be comforted"
(Matt. 5:4, niv). *Blessed* means favored, happy, esteemed, hon-
ored, and prosperous.[10]

Mourning comes with a feeling of sadness from loss, but
regret from sin and the mistakes you have made can also bring
a sense of loss. You may have lost time, relationships, jobs, pets,
marriages, money, homes, and opportunities. Loss comes in
many different forms.

I once lost my laptop and grieved over it for days because
it had all my intellectual property on it—years and years of
research and notes. It was like losing a close relative. Plus, I
was on a deadline to submit a manuscript to my publisher. In
that transitional period of mourning, I felt a deep sense of
hopelessness and helplessness. I prayed to God and asked for
help. Though I was still in mental anguish, God came through
and gave me perspective. With His help I was able to write
an even better manuscript. I recovered what was lost because
I placed my hope in God. Hope comes when you give up your
need to understand and begin instead to depend on God. Total
dependence on God gives birth to faith.

We lose our hope in situations when we are unable to see
how God is working or can work in the midst of them. David's
mighty men lost hope in him when they came home from
a battle to discover their city ravaged and their loved ones

kidnapped. I can only image how David felt. On the one hand, he had every right to be celebrating. But then, on the heels of one of his greatest victories, he returns home to total devastation. What did David do?

> David enquired at the LORD, saying, Shall I pursue after this troop? Shall I overtake them? And he answered him, Pursue: for thou shalt surely overtake them, and without fail recover all.
>
> —1 SAMUEL 30:8

I decree in this season of your life, no matter what you are confronted with, you will not give in to the seduction of throwing in the towel. I declare that you are in a recovery mode. Everything you lost will be recovered. You will recover from the loss of your:

- job
- marriage
- health
- finances
- faith
- hope
- dreams
- car
- house

- children

- salvation

- direction

David received this word from the Lord in a place called Ziklag, which in Hebrew means "winding."[11] It suggests something that is twisting, not straight or straightforward. Life takes us on a lot of twists and turns; it is not always straightforward or simple. Hope will give you the inspiration and motivation you need to keep going when you feel like giving up. I pray you will never lose the ability to hope in the midst of life's detours. I speak hope into your soul and faith into your spirit. Faith mixed with hope looks ahead and anticipates a brighter future.

ACTIVATE YOUR FAITH

Sometimes as we travel through life, we hit bends in the road and blind spots where visibility is minimal. We don't always know how to proceed. This is why faith in God is important. Faith is the GPS that will guide you. Looking ahead in faith gives closure to what is in the past. The apostle Paul instructed, "Put off your old self" (Eph. 4:22, NIV). He reminds you that "forgetting what is behind and straining toward what is ahead" (Phil. 3:13, NIV) is the task of every disciple. Forgetting does not imply that the memory disappears altogether. It means that all emotional and spiritual attachments to something or someone are severed so that they no longer tug at you or dominate your thoughts.

Endings require you to pronounce an end to self-sufficiency

and by faith totally depend on God, believing that God is not only able to do above and beyond what you are able to imagine, but that He is able to do *all things* through His mighty power actively working within you. As Paul wrote to the Ephesians, God "is able to do exceedingly abundantly above all that we ask or think, according to the power that works in us" (Eph. 3:20, NKJV). God is not in the business of meeting our expectations but exceeding them!

Genesis 1:2 explains how the Spirit of God moved in the midst of a chaotic and confusing state. Likewise, in the midst of your chaos and confusion the Spirit of God is present. "So do not fear," wrote the prophet Isaiah, "for I am with you; do not be dismayed, for I am your God. I will strengthen you and help you; I will uphold you with my righteous right hand" (Isa. 41:10, NIV). God's Spirit has been given to you as a gift, not only to show you things to come, but also to give you the faith to believe when all hope seems lost. Your job is to "only believe" by activating the faith you have—to stand in the midst of any circumstance and declare what you need illuminated, just as God declared, "Let there be light" (Gen. 1:3).

Any transformation, any change or transition, requires faith. People of faith don't just prophesy to their future; they provoke it. Faith takes you into the realm of unlimited possibilities. Faith sees what other people overlook.

After a troubled childhood and then a stint in the Army, Harry Wayne Huizenga moved to Florida where he saw a business opportunity. He bought a truck and started collecting garbage in Broward County. In less than ten years Huizenga owned a fleet of garbage trucks that worked across Florida and eventually across all of the United States as Waste Management.

But Huizenga didn't stop there. One of his friends mentioned a company named Blockbuster, and after visiting one of its stores, Huizenga decided to buy it. He turned Blockbuster into another nationwide company, which he eventually sold to Viacom for more than eight billion dollars. But Huizenga didn't stop there. He launched three more Fortune 500 companies and owned three professional sports teams.[12]

Huizenga's younger years were difficult. His father was abusive, and his parents' marriage was volatile. But instead of being negatively affected by his family's situation, he started where he was with what he had and used it as motivation to push himself further, ultimately reaching back to improve the welfare of his entire family.[13] He took one small step at a time, beginning with being willing to pick up the trash. And so it must be with you.

Although Huizenga's is a modern-day story, the destinies of many biblical characters were altered by a single small step as well. Rahab, Ruth, David, and many others started where they were with what they had, often in dark circumstances— and now you know their names and their stories. Have faith in God, but also have faith in who God created you to be. In moving on from where you are, take small steps of faith and live one day at a time. "Do not despise these small beginnings, for the LORD rejoices to see the work begin" (Zech. 4:10, NLT).

Start where you are with what you have. Be faithful with whatever little you've got. "If you are faithful in little things, you will be faithful in large ones" (Luke 16:10, NLT). Take one small step at a time.

Don't be fooled by what others think is worthless garbage. That garbage could be worth millions, if not billions of dollars. Learn to leverage what might seem like waste in your life. God Himself is in the waste management business. He never wastes one of our foibles or fumbles. He uses them all, turning our messes into masterpieces.

GET LIGHT AND SPEAK LIGHT

In Genesis 1:2 as God's Spirit was "brooding over the dark vapors" (TLB), God spoke and said, "Let there be light" (v. 3, NIV). Light exposes things that are otherwise undetectable. As human beings, we are often blinded by our circumstances and the emotions attached to them. Because light was the first thing God created, it should be the first thing you seek or speak when you find yourself "brooding over the dark vapors" of your life.

Don't make a move until you get God's light on it. Light comes as wisdom, knowledge, discernment, revelation, insight, hindsight, foresight, and vision. Light comes in the form of God's Word: "Your word is a lamp to my feet and a light to my path" (Ps. 119:105, NKJV) and "The entrance of Your words gives light; it gives understanding to the simple" (v. 130, NKJV). Shine God's Word on it.

Then speak God's Word, which is like speaking light. Light changes the atmosphere, and so do the words of God. What have you put into the atmosphere? Faith must be spoken for it to be released as a force. Many situations require prayer, but some situations need you to speak to them. Faith moves you from talking about your situation to speaking to your situation.

> Jesus answered and said to them, "Have faith in God. For assuredly, I say to you, whoever says to this mountain, 'Be removed and be cast into the sea,' and does not doubt in his heart, but believes that those things he says will be done, he will have whatever he says."
> —MARK 11:22–23, NKJV

A mountain is a metaphor for things that are impossible to change, adjust, or move. Yet Jesus instructs us to speak to those proverbial mountains. Once you believe, you must speak! "'I believed; therefore, I have spoken.' Since we have that same spirit of faith, we also believe and therefore speak" (2 Cor. 4:13, NIV). The Bible says that when you believe, you speak what you believe. According to Romans 10:10, "For with the heart one believes unto righteousness, and with the mouth confession is made unto salvation" (NKJV). Your mouth is powerful, "For by your words you will be justified, and by your words you will be condemned" (Matt. 12:37, NKJV).

Start where you are by speaking light into your situation. Start where you are right now by declaring where you want to be. Speak to your circumstances. Speak what you believe about what is possible (or speak about it until you believe it)! Speak the Word! It will light your way forward.

> You will also declare a thing, and it will be established for you; so light will shine on your ways.
> —JOB 22:28, NKJV

- ◆ ◆ ◆ -

CHAPTER 3

Separate, Separate, Separate

THE LAW OF SANCTIFICATION

And God divided the light from the darkness.
And God called the light Day, and the
darkness he called Night. And the evening
and the morning were the first day.
—GENESIS 1:4–5

WHEN GOD SPOKE light into existence, the darkness did not disappear. God, however, divided the light from the darkness, and He expects you to do the same. This separation between light and dark is a fundamental principle in the kingdom and a powerful theme throughout the Bible.

In Genesis 12:1 the Lord told Abram, "Go from your country, your people and your father's household to the land I will show you" (NIV). God was separating Abram from his native culture for a special work. When God returned the Israelites to the Promised Land after their Babylonian exile, the prophet Ezra told them, "Do his will and separate yourselves from the people living around you" (Ezra 10:11, NCV). He did not want the people to fall back into the same sins that led them into exile in the first place.

In the New Testament, Paul wrote to the Corinthians, "Do not be yoked together with unbelievers. For what do righteousness and wickedness have in common? Or what fellowship can light have with darkness?" (2 Cor. 6:14, NIV). Quoting from Isaiah and Ezekiel, Paul reminded them, "Come out from them and be separate, says the Lord. Touch no unclean thing, and I will receive you." (v. 17, NIV).

Are there areas in your life in which God is calling you to be set apart and separated? Take a candid look at what you have allowed to cast a shadow in your life, your mind, or your heart. Look to the source of all light, the One in whom we know "there is no darkness at all" (1 John 1:5, NIV) and "no variation or shadow of turning" (Jas. 1:17, NKJV). When you are struggling with uncertainty or confusion, clearly separate within yourself what is of God and what is not.

Saying "Goodbye, yesterday!" is a daily practice. Learn to distinguish between light and dark; clearly separate the two in your beliefs, habits, and thought patterns. This requires both discernment and discipline. Interestingly, *discernment* comes from the Latin root meaning "to separate, set apart, divide."[1] Every day you must start anew by choosing to put first things first, realigning your thoughts and actions toward where you want to be and separating yourself from those things that run counter to your higher purpose.

SEPARATE THE SPIRITUAL FROM THE PHYSICAL

Separation can take many forms and produce different types of fruit. For example, separation from injustice is righteousness; separation from sin is holiness; separation from distraction is dedication; and separation from indulgence is consecration. Separation can mean being spiritually or emotionally separated rather than physically separated. It can involve the discipline of redirecting your thoughts away from worldly distractions, thereby sanctifying your soul.[2]

Spiritual disciplines draw you closer to God, and the closer you move toward God, the more you set yourself apart from the temptations of the enemy and the flesh. The first step in separating yourself from sin, the cares of this world, materialistic thinking and attitudes, carnal appetites, or excess of any kind, is to draw closer to God.

If you want to get unstuck, practice holy separation. This is how you maintain your spiritual, mental, and physical health. Fasting in its many forms is valuable for this separation. For instance, you can fast food or television intermittently or for a set period of time. This will not only help you be more mindful but will also help you become more God-minded. Separation will empower you to move forward simply by disengaging you from the things that hold you back. As the author of Hebrews writes, "Let us throw off everything that hinders and the sin that so easily entangles" (12:1, NIV). Another version says, "Let us strip off every weight that slows us down, especially the sin that so easily trips us up" (NLT). Doing that helps us "run with perseverance the race marked out for us" (v. 1, NIV).

SEPARATE FROM DISTRACTIONS

There is a race marked out for you. You, the runner, are ready to race between the clearly marked lines. You can't move forward unless you are facing forward. Blinders worn by racehorses keep them from looking to either side and getting distracted so they don't bolt in fear in another direction. Some of you need those types of blinders so you don't avert your gaze and veer off course in a panic. Keep your focus directed forward. How can you run to obtain that prize if you are always looking over your shoulder? Keep focused on what is ahead of you as you "press on toward the goal for the prize" (Phil. 3:14, NKJV).

SEPARATE BY LEANING ON GOD

While separation is a process of breaking free from distractions, it also means not becoming overly attached to outcomes. Separation in this sense is a form of detachment. When you are attached to a certain result, you become fearful and insecure. Attachment is a form of poverty consciousness that will direct your focus to what is not working or lead you to become anxious about potentially negative outcomes. This is not faith, but rather is taking things into your own hands and leaning on your limited understanding, which is often rooted in a scarcity mindset. Instead, let go and lean on God. Emotionally detach from any preconceived idea of how things should be. This type of detachment leads to a wealth consciousness, the abundant life Christ spoke of in John 10:10. Trust God with the outcome. This leads to the liberty you find when you consecrate yourself to God's will for your life.

SEPARATE YOUR THOUGHTS

Getting a grip on your life and activating the power of God within you requires that you act from the mind of Christ and not your feelings. You will have to differentiate between thoughts sourced in the kingdom of light and those emanating from the kingdom of darkness. Paul instructs us to "demolish arguments and every pretension that sets itself up against the knowledge of God," and to "take captive every thought to make it obedient to Christ." (2 Cor. 10:5, NIV).

First, you have to be discerning, and then you must exercise the power of your will to separate yourself from every evil thing. You must choose blessing or cursing, death or life, and "choose for yourselves this day whom you will serve" (Josh 24:15, NIV). Draw boundaries when it comes to how you will walk out your faith and values, those with whom you will associate, and even where you will place your attention. Be the person who is "putting aside all malice and all deceit and hypocrisy and envy and all slander" (1 Pet. 2:1, NASB), having "nothing to do with unclean and foolish stories" (1 Tim. 4:7, BBE).

THE LAW OF SANCTIFICATION

The Greek word *hagiazō*, which means to "separate from profane things,"[3] is translated into English as *sanctify*. The process of sanctification is what the Holy Spirit does in your life as He "works in you both to will and to do for His good pleasure" (Phil. 2:13, NKJV). Sanctification is the ongoing process of being separated and set apart for the purposes of God.

Once you are spiritually saved through Christ, you must

continue to "work out your salvation" (v. 12, NIV) to "the salvation of your souls" (1 Pet. 1:9, NKJV). It is up to you to set
yourself apart from sins that "war against the soul" (1 Pet. 2:11,
NKJV) and separate you from God. You must "abstain from
every form of evil" (1 Thess. 5:22, NKJV) that extinguishes the
Holy Spirit's presence from your life and "take captive every
thought to make it obedient to Christ" (2 Cor. 10:5, NIV).

Engineer and professor Henry Morris, PhD, wrote, "Even
though we have been given a new nature of light, the old
nature of darkness is still striving within, and we have to be
exhorted: 'For ye were sometimes darkness, but now are ye
light in the Lord: walk as children of light' (Ephesians 5:8)."[4]
It is all too easy to look at your life, believing that your current state of affairs is proof that nothing is working out for you.
But more than likely, you're simply not walking in the light.
Instead, you are walking "according to the flesh," which is what
Paul warns against in his letter to the Galatians (4:29, NKJV).
"For the flesh sets its desire against the Spirit, and the Spirit
against the flesh; for these are in opposition to one another"
(Gal. 5:17, NASB). You must separate what is of the Spirit and
what is of your carnal nature, becoming mindful of what you
do proactively from a position of faith versus what you do reac-
tively out of fear.

The Holy Spirit works in your life to gently convict you
regarding those areas you need to sanctify in order to grow.
Sometimes you need a call to wake up from your sleep (Eph.
5:14) and renew your mind (Rom. 12:2). While you are tempted
to place your confidence and security in beauty and material
wealth, difficult circumstances can shake you free from that

which hinders your growth. This process of sanctification is not always comfortable, but God works in you because of His love for you. And you can be assured that He will never allow you to be tempted beyond what you can stand, and "when you are tempted, he will show you a way out so you can endure" (1 Cor. 10:13, NLT).

Sanctification is not about living a perfect, sinless life. "We all fall short of God's glorious standard" (Rom. 3:23, NLT). The apostle John wrote, "If we say we have no sin, we deceive ourselves, and the truth is not in us" (1 John 1:8, ESV). It is not your own effort that sanctifies you, but you are to pursue sanctification in humility and obedience so you may grow in Christ.

After you wake up as you are urged to do in Ephesians 5, you are to "walk circumspectly, not as fools but as wise, redeeming the time, because the days are evil" (vv. 15–16, NKJV). How do you do this? You must "understand and firmly grasp what the will of the Lord is" (v. 17, AMP). You must "study to shew thyself approved...rightly dividing the word of truth" (2 Tim. 2:15). This is the primary means of the ongoing sanctification process for the born-again believer: "Sanctify them by the truth. Your word is truth" (John 17:17, NKJV). We are sanctified "by the washing with water through the word" (Eph. 5:26, NIV).

The Bible is the source of God's sanctifying word of truth. Hebrews 4:12 tells us that "The word of God is alive and active. Sharper than any double-edged sword, it penetrates even to dividing soul and spirit, joints and marrow; it judges the thoughts and attitudes of the heart" (NIV). Sanctification is experiential; it produces new, divine, holy impulses. The Christian life is a continual process of encouraging the new life and denying the old. We grow and mature through the power of the Spirit, through applying God's Word, and with the help of God's grace.

ESTABLISH CLEAR BOUNDARIES

The most powerful practice you can put into place to reframe your reality is establishing healthy boundaries. I grew up one of seven children in a tiny, overcrowded house. We shared everything, from dresser space to sleeping three to a bed. I learned the importance of marking out my boundaries at an early age. Beyond the obvious physical and psychological boundaries, I had to figure out where I ended and someone else began—what truly was my concern and priority and what belonged to my siblings. Their urgencies and priorities were not always mine. Their fights and disagreements were not mine.

I had to learn the skill of not getting entangled in "group think" and to maintain my individuality. Today this skill is necessary for all believers. Paul instructs us to "be not conformed to this world: but be ye transformed by the renewing of your mind, that ye may prove what is that good, and acceptable, and perfect, will of God" (Rom. 12:2). This takes the ability to discern your priorities by getting clarity on God's plan for your life. When you get clear on His plans for you, you are able to determine what the non-negotiables in your life should be and thus draw a clear line in the sand as to what you will get involved with and what you will not.

Time is an important commodity, and you cannot afford to waste time on the temporal, trivial, and unimportant. God has given each one of us sufficient time to accomplish everything

He has assigned for us to accomplish. When you waste your time, or allow others to waste it, you can never get it back. You don't have to go through life regretting things you could have done but didn't because of time wasters or time-wasting activities. Distinguish between the important and the unimportant—and make the important your priority.

I was the first in my family to become a born-again Christian. For me, studying the Word of God became my top priority. Since then, I have always carved out substantial time in my busy and demanding schedule to make time to be in the Word first thing every single day. The Word of God is sanctifying and cleansing (Eph. 5:26). You could even say it's detoxifying. The Word of God feeds and nourishes my soul. Studying the Word is more important to me than breakfast or a shower.

In order for me to have time in the Word, I have to establish time and mental boundaries that determine what I will make time to do and what I will not allow to disturb me. My boundary determines when I get out of bed so I have sufficient time to study and meditate on God's Word. This is the most important boundary I can recommend that you establish in your own life, whether you are struggling to bounce back from a setback, or well on your way to achieving your dreams. Carving out that time first thing each day is the most valuable thing you can do for your spiritual, mental, emotional, relational, and even physical health.

You will need to establish clear boundaries like this in every area of your life. If you have read my book *Hello, Tomorrow!*, you will be familiar with the twelve areas that comprise your life compass, which is a way to focus your vision and stay guided in the direction you want to go. I encourage you to get a copy of *Hello, Tomorrow!* and read chapter eight. There I reference Buckminster Fuller's twelve degrees of freedom as a metaphorical representation of how you can create synergy around twelve areas that make up the directional points on your life compass. These twelve areas are significant to maximizing your full potential in the most healthy, holistic manner.

Of course, it helps if you have already done the vision work in each area, but today I want you to reflect on the areas that follow and ask the Holy Spirit to show you where you need to draw some boundaries. What do you need to separate from in each area to garner greater forward momentum? What are some disciplines you need to establish that will help you get unstuck wherever you're not seeing the results you've envisioned?

This would be a good time to get your journal out and do some writing. The prompts are only suggestions to help you get started.

1. Your personal brand

This is "people's perception of and emotional attachment to the image that comes to their minds when they think of you."[5]

- What might you need to separate from to protect your brand reputation?

- How can you exercise more discernment when it comes to opportunities and threats?

2. Companionship/marriage

- What thought or behavior patterns erode the health of your primary relationship?

- Consider how you might set apart not only more time, but more energy for your loved one.

3. Family (immediate and extended)

- What is keeping you from engaging more deeply with your family?

- Do you need to eliminate some toxic emotions regarding a family member?

4. Personal growth and development

- What is keeping you from maximizing your personal potential?

- Do you need to reevaluate habits or routines in order to accelerate your personal growth?

5. Career/calling

- How clearly are you discerning your calling in this season?

- What daily disciplines will propel you forward in your career?

6. Friends/colleagues

- Do you need to separate from any friends or associates for a season?

- Are there any thoughts or words you need to eliminate regarding a friend or colleague?

7. Networks/alliances/partnerships

- Might you need to realign your priorities in order to invest in the growth of your network?

- Should you walk away from any alliances or partnerships?

8. Recreation and renewal

- What is getting in the way of your taking more time to re-create and renew?

- How can you readjust your schedule?

9. Spiritual growth and development

- Do you set aside time each day to invest in your spiritual growth?

- How should you put an end to any sinful thoughts or behaviors?

10. Financial stability

- Do you need to rein in certain spending habits?

- Have you faithfully set apart your tithe?

11. Health, wellness, and fitness

- Should you separate from any foods or beverages?

- Do you exercise daily?

- Do you go to sleep at a reasonable time?

12. Legacy

- What do you need to do less of now that will enable you to do more later?

- Are you setting apart time and/or money to invest in the next generation?

Sometimes it's not a matter of needing to do more in the various areas of our lives but discerning what you need to eliminate. Take a candid look at what might be more of a distraction than a benefit. Every garden needs to be weeded, and every home can use a good decluttering. Say goodbye to whatever isn't serving you or is no longer serving you in this season.

No matter your starting point when you picked up this book, you can turn things around beginning today. You can end well by setting yourself apart and allowing God to "sanctify you through and through" (1 Thess. 5:23, NIV). The power of Holy Spirit is always available to you.

You create a new beginning whenever you submit to God and decide to seek Him first because what begins with God will end right. Ask Him to help you divide the light from the dark in your life and to call into existence whatever you need to usher in a clear new day.

> May God Himself, the God of peace, sanctify you through and through. May your whole spirit, soul, and body be kept blameless.
> —1 THESSALONIANS 5:23, NIV

PART TWO

— • • • —

Recharge

• • •

CHAPTER 4

Bring Order To Your Life

THE LAW OF ORDER

Then God said, "Let the waters under the
heavens be gathered together into one place,
and let the dry land appear"; and it was so.
And God called the dry land Earth, and the
gathering together of the waters He called
Seas. And God saw that it was good.
—GENESIS 1:9–10, NKJV

TRAVEL A LOT, and once when I approached the arrival gate,
I witnessed a bit of a ruckus—shouting, cheers, and whistles.
A man's large family was welcoming that fellow traveler home.
He was laden down with a carry-on, a suit bag, and a coat.
Little children ran up to him and wrapped their arms around
his legs, insisting that he pick them up. But instead of drop-
ping the baggage, he raised his laden arms up and proclaimed,
"I can't because my hands are full."

At that point I had an epiphany. Most people cannot embrace

their amazing future because they refuse to let go of the baggage they're carrying! Getting rid of your baggage requires you to surrender some things. Many people struggling to gain control of their lives cling to things they should really be letting go. Out of fear or desperation, they won't let go of the familiar or surrender the past in order to grab hold of the future. I understand, because sometimes letting go feels like falling hopelessly through the air or sinking rapidly to the bottom of the ocean.

Do you remember those monkey bars on your childhood playground? The bars were spaced just far enough apart that to grab onto the next one, you had to completely let go of the first one. It took a tremendous amount of willpower and faith to be suspended in the air for a split second as you swung toward the next bar. In the same way, if you're going swing into your future, you must garner the faith to let go of what you're clinging to—all your justifications and excuses.

God has fashioned you with the kind of springiness that allows you to move through the air, so to speak, or dive deep into God's promises. You have been genetically designed for life in the kingdom, for a life of faith that defies the odds. You have the resilience you need to overcome any challenge or stress you encounter in this life on earth.

LEARN TO LET GO

"Get yourself together" is a phrase that many of us have heard at one point or another. But getting yourself together actually starts when you disconnect from things and people that keep you attached to a lifestyle or culture you have outgrown—when you discard certain behaviors and habits that keep you connected to an old mindset, an old season, or an old paradigm. It requires divesting yourself of certain things that keep you tied to your past so you can adequately prepare for your future.

A soldier named Mike was returning from the Korean War. Mike stood on the stern of the ship at twilight trying to imagine what life would be like back in the States. Soon he started noticing things floating in the water, but he couldn't quite make out what they were. Then, one thing flew through the air, whooshing by him and splash-landing in the ocean. Then another flew by, and another. Suddenly he realized these were shoes, socks, shirts, coats, undershorts, canteens, and mess gear—things his fellow soldiers were throwing overboard. Everyone longed for a new beginning. As much as was humanly possible, those soldiers were letting go of what defined their past.[1]

FLEX YOUR SPIRITUAL MUSCLES

Deep in the ocean, one of nature's most flexible mammals thrives. Despite crushing water pressure, sperm whales feed off giant squid that live seven thousand feet below the surface. Their secret is their flexibility. At such depths, water pressure would break the ribs of most mammals and collapse their lungs. However, the bendable cartilage that connects the ribs of these whales allows their rib cages to collapse some under the pressure. Instead of snapping, their ribs flex.[2] Through divine engineering, God built flexibility into their DNA, and thus whales are able to feast on giant squid that live near the ocean floor. What has God designed for you to feast on?

It's time for you to flex your spiritual muscles so you can

feast on God's blessings. It's time to do a deep dive and rid yourself of all the things that have kept you from rising above your circumstances and have caused you to feel overwhelmed with life. Adaptation stems from resilience, which is essential for thriving both in the natural world as well as in your daily spiritual life. God has given you authority over all power of the enemy, and therefore you already have the competitive advantage. Go deep into the Word of God and access the power of God that dwells in you, for "greater is he that is in you, than he that is in the world" (1 John 4:4).

God's power allows you to overcome the most crushing circumstances. Life has a way of hitting us so hard that if it were not for God's power within, we would all break under its pressure. His presence in your life brings the rock-solid faith you need to overcome your greatest challenges. I know of so many people who drown in pain and break under pressure. These folks turn to drugs and alcohol as a means to survive. You don't have to go through life in survival mode. The power of God in you mixed with your faith will help you thrive. Your days of surviving are over. I decree that you will thrive. Not only that, I decree that your business, ideas, ministry, marriage, children, and health will thrive.

Even as God called the earth from out of the waters, He is calling you from out of your past. By His Spirit you are empowered with faith to overcome, but you must activate that faith by the words you speak. The Bible says, "They overcame him by the blood of the Lamb, and by the word of their testimony" (Rev. 12:11). Nothing built on the Word can fall apart. Your life should be lived by the Word of God. Your lifestyle should epitomize the Word of God. Your prayers should be driven by the Word of God. Your success should be determined by the Word of God. Your business and ministries should be sustained by the Word of God. Your children should progress by the Word of God.

To build your spiritual capacity, you must increase your resilience to negative situations and build your spiritual immunity to the "dis-ease" caused by fear and anxiety. The key to building greater resiliency is to continually speak God's Word over your circumstances. This is how you adapt to the pressures of the deep.

In addition to increasing your spiritual resilience, adaptability empowers you to strive for goals that would normally intimidate you. To embrace these challenges, you must bring order to your thoughts and to how you spend your time. Most people use their time to worry or plot and plan their revenge. But that is a waste of your time. God called the earth from out of the waters, which is tantamount to bringing the solidity of your faith in God into the equation of your life. Like a mountain rising up from the sea, may God give you mountain-moving (or rising-up) faith.

> Have faith in God. For verily I say unto you, That whosoever shall say unto this mountain, Be thou removed, and be thou cast into the sea; and shall not doubt in his heart, but shall believe that those things which he saith shall come to pass; he shall have whatsoever he saith.
> —MARK 11:22–23

THERE IS GREATNESS IN YOU

You have greatness in you. Dare to do great things with your life. No one becomes great by staying the same. Use adaptability to push your limits and discover untapped potential. Who knows what rewards you will reap if you are willing to risk change!

Change for the better begins with the way you think about the time God has given you on this earth. Too many people walk around confused about how to bring their vision to pass, what to do next, or how to overcome setbacks and conquer the emotions attached to disappointments, loss, and pain. Your thoughts are the key to living the life God promised you.

You are transformed by the renewing of your mind (Rom. 12:2). Jesus said, "I am come that they might have life, and that they might have it more abundantly" (John 10:10). God wants you to live in abundance, and that abundance includes abundant health, friendships, opportunities, joy, peace, and happiness. Your abundant thoughts provide the foundation for an abundant life. Consider what author and pastor Rick Warren says about the power of your thoughts: "To change your life, you must change the way you think. Behind everything you do is a thought. Every behavior is motivated by a belief, and every action is prompted by an attitude. "Be careful how you think; your life is shaped by your thoughts."[3]

How are your own thoughts, beliefs, and attitudes keeping you from embracing change?

Every day God gives each person opportunities to advance His kingdom. Ecclesiastes 9:11 states that He gives all of us time and opportunity: "The race is not to the swift or the battle to the strong, nor does food come to the wise or wealth to the brilliant or favor to the learned; but time and chance happen to them all" (NIV). The key to making the most of every opportunity is *firmly grasping the will of the Lord.* This is why it is vitally important to renew your mind continually with the Word of God. Every moment of the day you must align your thoughts and words with God's thoughts and Word.

Stop being wishy-washy with what you believe. Be as solid and steadfast as the earth. Don't let the devil cause you to question the faithfulness of God. Even as the earth gives you something solid to stand upon, so does your faith in God. Jesus gave you a fundamental key to successfully commanding every situation when He told you in John 15:7, "If you abide in Me, and My words abide in you, you will ask what you desire, and it shall be done for you" (NKJV).

This is why God instructs you to meditate on "the Word of God, which is effectually at work in you who believe [exercising its superhuman power in those who adhere to and trust in and rely on it]" (1 Thess. 2:13, AMPC). God's Word is life and health to those who find it (Prov. 4:20–22).

THE LAW OF ORDER

Your future comes one day at a time. The present is God's gift to you, and how you use it is your gift to Him. Time management is not about stuffing all the activities you can into a twenty-four-hour day. "Time management" is a misnomer because technically you cannot manage time. Instead, you can manage your activities according to specific time frames, which is the art of making every moment of every day count.

Ordering your day requires you to discern between what is distracting busywork and what is kingdom business. Effective time management requires getting God's heart on what is worth *investing* time in versus what you should not be *spending* or even *wasting* time doing. Ensure that every action, every thought, and every word is in alignment with your divine purpose and God's will as found His Word. We find a foundational key regarding this principle in Paul's letter to the Ephesians:

> Look carefully then how you walk! Live purposefully and worthily and accurately, not as the unwise and witless, but as wise (sensible, intelligent people), making the very most of the time [buying up each opportunity], because the days are evil. Therefore, do not be vague and thoughtless and foolish, but understanding and firmly grasping what the will of the Lord is.
>
> —Ephesians 5:15–17, ampc

As with any financial investment, you must ask what kind of return your time investments are yielding. Time *spent* is a cost, and you must be mindful of the benefit you are exchanging for the cost you are incurring.

God provided the ultimate example of effective time management and order in the Book of Genesis. In six days He created the earth and everything in it, and on the seventh day He rested. God created everything in a planned order, developing each organism and species in His designed progression. God did not waste His resources, especially His time. It all went according to plan. He was purposeful and concise as He unveiled life on our planet.

Here we are introduced to the third day. It was on this day that God commanded the earth to emerge as He gathered the waters. With three words, "Let there be," there was. By your words, bring order to your thoughts and order to your life. Stop using your time to complain, bellyaching about what you don't want. Command your day by commanding your morning. Declare what you want rather than complain about what you don't have.

REORDER YOUR DAY

In Genesis 1:9–10 the land was appointed a particular place in the cosmos. Don't miss this point: Everything in the universe has a place. This is the precursor to order. Do not miss out on the rewards that come with bringing order to every area of your life and the environment in which you live and work. Order is what gives you the freedom to be creative. Order gives you the peace of mind you need to tune into God's supernatural frequencies and tap into divine inspiration. Don't let your day control you; control your day. You can do this with order. Without order you will be distracted with the cares and concerns of this life so that you cannot still your mind to listen to God. Hear God's voice saying to you this day, "Let all things be done decently and in order" (1 Cor. 14:40).

Order is not about adding more things to your to-do list. This will only add more stress to your life. It is impossible to imagine the possibilities or envision alternative outcomes when you are overextended and stressed. You need to schedule time to purposefully paint the canvas of your life by investing in creative dreaming. Invest in time to think, to craft a vision of the life you want today and of the tomorrow you would like to live. Order that tomorrow in your mind. Visualize every detail it. Order your day so you have the time and space you need to place the brush strokes on the masterpiece God has pre-ordained for you. Make certain that you have scheduled time for praying, meditation, reading the Word of God, journaling, imagining, and worshipping God for all He makes possible. This is how you bring order to your day and to your life.

Learn the art of making every moment of every day count. Create specific daily, weekly, monthly, and yearly goals based on your personal vision for your life. If you need help in writing a vision, I have written an entire book that will help you called *Hello Tomorrow!* This requires skill and discipline. My first twenty-year vision took me about six months to write. Back in those days, there were no books that broke down the components I needed to focus on. In *Hello Tomorrow!* I have broken these components down for you.

Skill and discipline divide the successful and productive from the unsuccessful and unproductive. Once you have written out a vision for your life, you will be future focused. Being future focused will enable you to identify time wasters and time-wasting activities. Get rid of all the activities and interpersonal dealings that waste your time. Sever your relationship with distractions, which include people and activities that do not bring a return on your investment of time. Set actionable goals for your week that include daily devotionals, an exercise routine, and special projects. You have been given the opportunity to create a masterpiece with your life. You will not have better tomorrows if you don't make the most of your todays—and say goodbye to your yesterdays. Your vision will become a catalyst for letting go by faith and trusting God to lead you forward. Walking away from disappointment and heartache requires picking yourself up, dusting yourself off, and moving forward, even in a small way. Put one foot in front of the other, trusting that God will show you where to step. It is God, after all, who is ordering your steps (Ps. 37:23)—even rescuing you from missteps. "If he stumbles..." writes the psalmist, "God has a grip on his hand" (v. 24, MSG)

Yet even while He has fashioned your steps, it is up to you to order or fashion your day. We can learn to order our days according to His will by praying: "Teach us to number our days, that we may gain a heart of wisdom" (Ps. 90:12, NIV). There is wisdom in the rhythms and routines you establish in your daily life. This is why I wrote *Commanding Your Morning*. But for you to command your day, you must first have a vision, and that is why I wrote *Hello, Tomorrow!*

To bring that vision to pass, you must learn the laws of faith, and that is why you are reading this book. It requires faith to reorder your life. It requires faith to speak order into the chaos of your circumstances. Today, in faith, I speak order into your life, ministry, finances, relationships, health, and all things concerning you.

> For everything there is a season, and a time for every matter under heaven.
>
> —ECCLESIASTES 3:1, ESV

◆ ◆ ◆

Choose Potential Over Problems

THE LAW OF POTENTIAL

And God said, Let the earth bring forth grass, the
herb yielding seed, and the fruit tree yielding fruit
after his kind, whose seed is in itself, upon the
earth: and it was so. And the earth brought forth
grass, and herb yielding seed after his kind, and
the tree yielding fruit, whose seed was in itself,
after his kind: and God saw that it was good. And
the evening and the morning were the third day.
—GENESIS 1:11–13

AT THE AGE of sixteen, Winston Churchill already had a clear vision of his purpose. He and a friend were discussing their futures after chapel at school one Sunday night when Churchill spoke about what he could see. "This country will be subjected somehow, to a tremendous invasion, by what means

I do not know, but...I tell you I shall be in command of the defences of London, and I shall save London and England from disaster....In the high position I shall occupy, it will fall to me to save the Capital and save the Empire."[1] He knew he was born with the potential for greatness.

Where does this potential come from? It comes from the same source that made Mother Teresa leave her country to serve the indigent in India and that caused Rosa Parks to remain seated on that bus. It comes from the same place that caused Nelson Mandela to fight against apartheid after twenty-seven years of imprisonment and as an ex-convict to go on to become a great moral, visionary, and transformational world leader.

Greatness comes from the same place that caused Amelia Earhart to become the first woman to fly over the Atlantic Ocean and to make the journey alone. It comes from the same place that compelled Barack Obama to campaign for the presidency of the United States and become the first man of color to win. It comes from the same place that caused fifteen-year-old Pakistani Malala Yousafzai to take a bullet for the cause of girls' education. Malala said, "I don't want to be remembered as the girl who was shot. I want to be remembered as the girl who stood up."[2] It comes from the same place that took me from poverty and positioned me as a thought leader on a global stage. It comes from a seed of greatness.

THE POWER OF THE SEED[3]

Each of us has incredible gifts and talents given to us by God that must be cultivated. Just as in Genesis 1, the tree yielded fruit with seed in it (v. 12), you, as a tree of righteousness, already have the seeds of incredible purpose, destiny, and greatness within you. These are seeds of the fruitfulness you were created to bear as a tree planted by God.

> They will be called oaks of righteousness, a planting of
> the LORD for the display of his splendor.
>
> —ISAIAH 61:3, NIV

A seed is a powerful metaphor for the force of potential you carry. The dictionary defines *potential* as "latent qualities or abilities that may be developed and lead to future success or usefulness."[4] Every seed has the innate, God-given potential to be greater than what it is, given the right environment. Likewise, everything in life is created with the potential to be greater than what it is when placed in a fertile environment.

Potential is what you can achieve but have not achieved yet. It is what you are gifted to build, paint, engineer, or write but have not yet envisioned. It is what you can own, sing, design, or drive but do not possess yet. Potential is what you have the seed in you for, but you have not yet accomplished.

Potential proves that nothing about your past defines you. No past experience has the power to destroy you, defeat you, deter you, or put an end to what you are capable of doing. In fact, your experiences revealed the hidden abilities within you that you wouldn't be aware of otherwise. They may have scared you, thrown you off balance, or temporarily devastated you, but they cannot erase your potential.

On the contrary, difficulties and challenges enlarge your capacity. Potential confirms that no matter what you have been through, you are not a victim. Something greater is ahead of you because you have yet to experience your greatest moment. You would not still be living if the setbacks and failures of yesterday were your ultimate defining moments. Potential says you still have greatness residing in you.

God sowed seed in you in the form of potential on the day you were conceived. Your seed is the divine energy of the Holy Spirit operating in the soil of your mind. Adam and Eve were born with this seed of potential. Adam used his potential to become the first zoologist because the demand activated the seed.

The seed of potential contains your divinely appointed but often unnoticed intelligence, skills, abilities, insights, proclivities, gifts, aptitudes, callings, capabilities, and talents that, when properly cultivated, bear the fruit of prosperity, progress, and success. So many people have the potential to be more, but they are not in the right environment. This seed will lay dormant until it is planted and cultivated in the right environment—until education, empowerment, and capacity-building processes expose it to the nutrients needed to grow.

You can recalibrate your environment beginning with your own mind by tilling the soil of your mental landscape. For example, if you would study in your field one hour a day, within a few short years, you would become an expert. That is cultivating your seed!

Nourish yourself to create the kind of fertile soul in which million-dollar ideas thrive. Pull up the weeds of doubt, fear, unbelief, envy, resentment, and insecurity. Plant the words of God about who you are in Christ. Plant your vision, hopes, and dreams. Then water it all with gratitude, praise, and worship.

Even as every natural seed has been given a specific purpose to fulfill and an invisible assignment to accomplish, you were born with a specific purpose and an assignment too. Purpose must be recognized, cultivated, and strategically planted in order for its divinely ordained potential to flourish and be maximized.

Sowing seed is not just about blessing your church, but also your family, community, industry, and region of the world. What skill, talent, idea, invention, or technological breakthrough has God given you to enhance and bless your neighborhood, your community, or your region? What has He given you to add value to your workplace, profession, marketplace, or field? Find the field He has given you and cultivate yourself in it. Then watch your family, community, business, and city thrive. You have something the world needs.

PROBLEMS AND PRESSURE BRING OUT POTENTIAL

God will plant you in a specific field and put pressure on you to maximize your potential and help you fulfill your assignment on the earth. What is the purpose of pressure and problems if not to expose the hidden potential within you?

Paul wrote to the Corinthians, "We are troubled on every side, yet not distressed; we are perplexed, but not in despair; Persecuted, but not forsaken; cast down, but not destroyed" (2 Cor. 4:8–9). Even as a seed must experience pressure and must push through the opposing forces of nature and gravity to grow, your seed will grow through the pressures and opposing forces of life. Problems do not come to destroy you, but to bring the best out of you, to activate your seed. They will unlock the potential, power, and life-giving force within you.

In Genesis 30 we read that Jacob was an entrepreneur who spent fourteen years submitted to institutionalized oppression from his uncle Laban. But Jacob cultivated that entrepreneurial seed as an employee until his entrepreneurial destiny was pressured to manifest itself by his frustrating circumstances. In the same way, your seed of greatness hidden within may require fierce opposition to break open and activate.

Wherever God plants you, He plans to prosper you. You are a seed God has strategically planted in the place, community, market, or sphere of influence in which you dwell so you can extend His kingdom in that place. The imagery of the seed shows you that you can rise up from your circumstances and bloom where you are planted. You don't need to be a victim when you know you have the potential to be greater than what you are at any given moment.

THE LAW OF POTENTIAL

When God created the universe, He downloaded the hidden seed of potential into everything. Potential is a divine law that states something has the innate ability to be greater than itself at any given moment. Greatness is in you; that's why you are never really satisfied with the status quo. The seed of greatness is the force that drives accomplishment. The seed of greatness is the catalyst for every great achievement. It makes you want more and pray for more.

Jabez had the potential to be greater than his capacity revealed and his culture dictated. He therefore prayed to God based on his perceived potential, "Oh, that You would bless me indeed, and enlarge my territory....So God granted him what he requested" (1 Chron. 4:10, NKJV). Jabez asked God to remove his self-imposed limitations, cultural restrictions, and an environment characterized by small-minded individuals. He asked God to enlarge his capacity, and God granted his request.

Deliberately move away from small thinking and ask God to give you the capacity to maximize your potential. Whatever you're currently thinking about doing, being, or acquiring, think bigger! Refuse to settle for good enough or average. To be average is to settle for a life governed by external forces and by limiting cultural and environmental restrictions.

The opposite of greatness is not inferiority but insignificance. It is settling for living a life of *average* simply because you refuse to challenge yourself to reach beyond the threshold of the familiar. Insignificance is choosing to live among the clutter of the common so you don't stick out among your friends for fear of being misjudged or misunderstood. It is knowing that you have it in you to do more and to be more but not having the courage to step out of the shadows of others, to defy the status quo, or to go out on a limb because you might fall or fail. Insignificance is refusing to realize that with God all things are possible. It is accepting *ordinary* as your life sentence. Insignificance is holding your gifts and abilities in witness protection and accepting the mediocre as God's standard.

An average mindset is the most destructive type of mentality because it is accepted by an anti-God culture that will never challenge you to expand your horizon, think outside the box, or defy the status quo. Mediocrity is popular because it requires no discipline. Eliminate your average mindset.

The realm of average is filled with faithless people who have given up on themselves, their dreams, and their vision. Pull away from this culture and ask God to help you dream again. Your future is filled with unlimited opportunities, and you have the potential to capitalize on each one that God presents on a daily basis. These opportunities are designed to stretch you and help you establish new goals while maximizing your potential in the process!

Some have mistaken average for being humble or content, but this is not accurate. Being average is failing to recognize that God created you in His image to be His representative. Most people decline their calling as His image-bearer simply because they fear being judged as arrogant or accused of thinking more highly of themselves than they ought.

Greatness is not about being better than someone else but being the best version of yourself. When you put your greatness on display, you glorify God! Resigning yourself to a life of underachievement with unfulfilled potential does not glorify God. You aren't an underachiever; you are an overcomer! You are capable of achieving so much more for God and His kingdom.

You serve a great God, and you can serve Him with the greatness seeded in you. He wants you to walk out your life in the fullness of that greatness. Whatever you focus on and truly desire, be it a vision, dream, or goal, you are well able to accomplish it.

If you were to actually see your potential from God's perspective, believing that He created you to be His representative in the earth, you would stop listening to what others think about you and instead start tapping into the hidden source of divine power. You would refuse to become a victim of circumstances or a product of your environment and instead view your challenges as divine catalysts that give rise to greater knowledge of your hidden potential.

It is not the vessel that makes its contents valuable, but the contents that makes the vessel valuable! Remember that the apostle Paul said, "We have this treasure in earthen vessels, that the excellency of the power may be of God, and not of us" (2 Cor. 4:7). God gave you as a gift to this world. Gifts should be treasured, so treasure what God has placed on the inside of you.

Potential is found in the strangest of places.

- For Rahab it was found living on Jericho's wall in the red-light district.

- For David it was found on in the fields among his flocks.

- For Moses it was found on the back side of a desert.

- For Joshua it was found in the midst of bereavement.

- For John the Revelator it was found on an isolated island.

- For Deborah it was found in a sexist field (the military).

- For Gideon it was found on the threshing floor.

- For Paul it was found as he lay blinded on the road to Damascus.

- For Joseph it was found in a prison.

- For Noah it was found in the midst of perversion and debauchery.

Where might your potential be found?

DON'T TAKE YOUR POTENTIAL TO THE GRAVE

"To each there comes in their lifetime a special moment when they are figuratively tapped on the shoulder and offered the chance to do a very special thing, unique to them, and fitted to their talents," a philosopher once observed, adding, "What a tragedy if that moment finds them unprepared or unqualified for that which could have been their finest hour."[5]

Could this be your defining moment? Today is the day you can choose to move beyond what was to what can be. Your dreams may have been delayed, but they are not denied. Your finest hour is on its way. You can tap into your potential to go further than you thought possible and accomplish more than you ever have before.

Greatness does not come from acting independently from God but from being fully dependent on Him and what you can do through Christ "because greater is he that is in you, than he that is in the world" (1 John 4:4). You serve a great God who wants to do great things through you because of the seed of potential He placed within you. You are born to be great! You are wired for greatness!

If Shakespeare had died before he wrote his poems and plays, the potential for *Hamlet*, *Macbeth*, and *Romeo and Juliet* would have been buried. Suppose Michelangelo had died before he painted the Sistine Chapel or Leonardo da Vinci had died before he painted the *Mona Lisa*. The beauty of their paintings would have been lost. Suppose Mozart had perished with all that music in his bosom. Had Moses passed away before encountering the burning bush, Israel might have remained in bondage.

If the apostle Paul had lost his life before meeting Jesus on the Damascus Road, the bulk of the New Testament might never have been written. If Abraham died before Isaac was born, the entire nation of Israel as we know it would never have existed. What if Martin Luther had passed from the earth without tacking his *Ninety-Five Theses* onto the door of the Wittenberg Castle Church? What if Charles Wesley had passed away without penning thousands of hymns or if John Wycliffe had died without organizing the first translation of the Bible into English? How different the history of the church would have been!

Can you imagine how many great works of art, music, and literature as well as how many medical and technological breakthroughs are buried in the graveyard near your house because people allowed someone else to dictate their future or restrict what they had the potential to do? People die with potential for greatness still buried within them, failing to access all that God had sown in them for the benefit of the world. Can you imagine how many solutions to problems we face today are buried with those whose lives are forever lost to the world?

You serve a great God who wants to make you great and do great things through you.

> Give us even more greatness than before.
> —PSALM 71:21, TPT

CHAPTER 6

• • •

Understand the Power of Time

THE LAW OF SEASONS

And God said, Let there be lights in the
firmament of the heaven to divide the day from
the night; and let them be for signs, and for
seasons, and for days, and years: and let them
be for lights in the firmament of the heaven
to give light upon the earth: and it was so.
—GENESIS 1:14–15

HAVE YOU EVER missed an opportunity? Maybe the deal of a lifetime presented itself, but you didn't recognize it. Perhaps the relationship you've always wanted or the access to the perfect platform came, but you somehow missed grabbing the opportunity. Maybe you missed doing that one thing that would have catalyzed the answer to that big prayer.

It could have been neglecting an important element that

would have changed the outcome of a project. Perhaps you didn't know how to take advantage of the potential for networking because you were operating with limited knowledge. Maybe you just missed a flight that caused you to miss an important appointment. Perhaps you were afraid to make a decision because of the inevitable fallout, so you did nothing.

Missed opportunities are so frustrating. Sometimes they don't look like what we expect, so we don't recognize them. Sometimes we are just not prepared for them and have to say no. For whatever reason, missing an opportunity is exasperating, especially if we notice God's divine timing in it.

When you miss the timing to do something, it may feel as if your life has spiraled out of control. But don't be discouraged because we have all done this at one time or another. That is one reason Jesus came as our Savior. God is the Redeemer of all things, even time. He will help restore what has been lost. Through the prophet Joel He promised, *"I will restore to you the years that the locust hath eaten, the cankerworm, and the caterpillar, and the palmerworm"* (Joel 2:25). God will reset the timing for you to fulfill your assignment.

TIME IS A DIVINE RESOURCE

God wants to give you wisdom for living, wisdom that is gained with time and experience. Time was one of the first things God created when He put the lights in the sky "for signs, and for seasons, and for days, and years" (Gen. 1:14). He created time *with* a purpose and *for* a purpose so that in time you can fulfill *your* purpose.

Since creating time was a priority for God, correctly using or allocating your time should be a priority for you. Understanding the value of time will have a profound effect on how you live day to day.

God gives you time while on earth to cultivate your seed of potential. He gives you time as a divine resource to prosper you if you properly value it and leverage the time and opportunities you have been given. If you don't, you will find yourself living a life impoverished by regrets. I believe Peter's admonition to "be sober, be vigilant" is in reference to how we steward our time in the midst of challenging moments, because squandering it makes you vulnerable to an enemy "seeking whom he may devour" (1 Pet. 5:8).

Time is an important heavenly commodity and the currency with which you trade on the earth. We are instructed by Paul in his letter to the Ephesians to redeem the time. "See then that you walk circumspectly, not as fools but as wise, redeeming the time, because the days are evil" (Eph. 5:15–16, NKJV). The enemy will approach you with distractions. This is why it is so important to diligently order your days. You must be vigilant in conferring with God concerning the timing of everything. God will "teach us to number our days, that we may apply our hearts unto wisdom" (Ps. 90:12).

I've heard it put something like this.

> To realize the value of one year, ask a student who has failed a few courses at university.
>
> To realize the value of one month, ask a mother who has given birth to a premature baby.
>
> To realize the value of one week, ask an editor of a weekly newspaper.

To realize the value of one day, ask a daily wage laborer who has kids to feed based on his ability to work.

To realize the value of one hour, ask the bride who is patiently waiting at the altar to meet her groom.

To realize the value of one minute, ask a person who has missed their connecting flight.

To realize the value of one second, ask a person who has avoided an accident.

To realize the value of one millisecond, ask the person who has won a silver medal in the Olympics.[1]

Learn the value of time. Give every day an assignment. Don't squander a single moment of this one precious life because within every moment is the potential to prosper and within every millisecond is an opportunity to win gold.

THE LAW OF SEASONS

Bigger than the subject of time is the Creator of time. God is the comptroller of time, the master designer, the manufacturer, and the engineer of time Himself. He still determines times and seasons. He has jurisdiction over when things begin and when those very things come to an end. God knows the purpose for your birth, the destiny for your life, and the trajectory necessary for you to arrive at your expected end. He knows what it will take to get you to live the vision He's inspired in your heart. It is God who has given you those desires in your heart, and it is God who will bring them to pass, if you delight yourself in Him (Ps. 37:4).

Take your mind off your current circumstances and fix your thoughts instead on the goodness and faithfulness of God (Col.

3:2). Trust Him to "make straight your paths" (Prov. 3:6, ESV) and lead you into the life of your dreams. Whatever it looks like in this season, it is just that—a season!

Everything under the sun operates according to seasons. The winter may feel cold and dark, but you know the spring will come. Even under the frozen ground, those seeds of potential are stirring, ready to break forth at the first sign of spring. "Look, the winter is past," wrote Solomon, "and the rains are over and gone. The flowers are springing up, the season of singing birds has come" (Song of Sol. 2:11–12, NLT). Because, wrote Solomon, "To every thing there is a season, and a time to every purpose under the heaven" (Eccles. 3:1).

Jesus told a parable about a fig tree that speaks of seasons:

> A man had a fig tree planted in his vineyard, and he came seeking fruit on it and found none. And he said to the vinedresser, "Look, for three years now I have come seeking fruit on this fig tree, and I find none. Cut it down. Why should it use up the ground?" And he answered him, "Sir, let it alone this year also, until I dig around it and put on manure. Then if it should bear fruit next year, well and good; but if not, you can cut it down."
>
> —LUKE 13:6–9, ESV

Something was prohibiting this fig tree from producing fruit. The owner of the vineyard gave it a specific time frame to grow and fulfill its assignment in the earth. The owner would come back every so often seeking its fruit, examining the tree to see whether it was fulfilling its assignment. However, year after year the tree had produced no sign of productivity, no proof that it was accomplishing its purpose, let alone maximizing its potential.

Like the fig tree, you are purposefully designed to bear fruit and to add value to a world hungry for solutions to its many crucial needs. Take account of your own fruitfulness. If you have been feeling stagnant and unsatisfied, you are probably not investing in others. If your life has been barren of good works, perhaps you should add fertilizer to your faith by meeting a need. There is nothing more satisfying than filling another's need. Nothing will get you back onto the path of your purpose more than serving others.

> For we are His workmanship, created in Christ Jesus for good works, which God prepared beforehand that we should walk in them.
>
> —EPHESIANS 2:10, NKJV

What are the good works God has prepared for you to do? God commissioned you to be fruitful, and until you find the fruit you are to bring forth into the earth, you will remain weak and sickly like the barren fig tree. James wrote, "Show me your faith without your works, and I will show you my faith by my works" (Jas. 2:18, NKJV).

Learn to make the most of the season you are in. Discern the times to understand what God is showing you today. The descendants of Issachar in 1 Chronicles 12:32 "were men that had understanding of the times, to know what Israel ought to do." What should you be doing in this season to position yourself for success in the next? What must you do now to be where you want to be this time next year? How can you begin being more productive now to till the soil of success in your garden of tomorrow?

Within the span of a season, everything about your life can be changed for the better. Sometimes change simply takes a new season, but more often it takes you plowing up the fallow ground, sowing new seeds, or fertilizing what has already been planted.

Most of us do not value the prospering power inherent in the season in which we find ourselves. Is it a time to plant, a time to weed, a time to water, or a time to reap? What book idea or business idea has been rolling around in your spirit? Is it time to hire a coach or contact an agent? Is it the season to initiate a new deal or open a new store? Or is it time to bring closure to a losing endeavor and walk away? Is it time to buy a new property or sell off what you have so you can move overseas to the mission field? Practice discernment. God will give you eyes to see whether the winter has past and it's time to plant or whether the fields are ripe for harvest. "And let us not grow weary while doing good, for in due season we shall reap if we do not lose heart" (Gal. 6:9, NKJV).

CULTIVATE YOUR TIME

You are the gardener of your time. You alone choose what to grow in the garden of your day, what to cultivate to produce the fruit you desire in the grand garden of your life. You have been given a lifetime to discover your purpose, to maximize your potential, and to leave a legacy for the next generation. Many great ones who have gone before you fulfilled their assignments in their lifetime, and God wants you to fulfill yours. He will give you strategies on how to use time to achieve your God-given dreams.

Know the value of time. If time is money, as is often said, then to waste time is to waste the opportunities given to you to create wealth. The Earl of Chesterfield said, "Know the true value of time; snatch, seize, and enjoy every moment of it. No idleness, no laziness, no procrastination; never put off till to-morrow what you can do to-day."[2] Imagine the possibilities that would emerge if you more masterfully leveraged the power of time, if you harnessed its power as the primary resource you have been given to create and cultivate whatever God has put in your hands. Just as a surfer gains speed and momentum from riding the waves of the ocean, you can skillfully "ride the waves" of the hours of your day.

We are all time travelers. From the day you were conceived until the day you die you are traveling through the seasons of time. Think about this truth for a moment: From your last birthday until your next, you will have completed a revolution around the sun without any effort or personal involvement. If you could accomplish such a feat without any planning or exertion, imagine what your life could be like 365 days from now with just a little focus and effort. Then imagine what would be possible if you gave each of those 365 days your undivided attention and the full force of your energy?

The word *undivided* means "not separated into parts or pieces: existing as a single whole."[3] It connotes being unbroken, uninterrupted, not distributed. It's true that you don't always have control over the circumstances and demands of the day, especially when children are involved. However, if you can command even a small portion of the day, a time when your attention is fully focused on a goal you are determined to achieve, you can accomplish extraordinary things.

EARLY TO BED, EARLY TO RISE

Harness the power of the last hour and the first hour of every day. You may not be able to control what unfolds in between, but you can generally regulate those. This may require you to stay up an hour later or wake up an hour earlier. But book-ending each end of your day with an hour to reflect, read, journal, and pray will supercharge every other hour you are awake. It was Martin Luther who said, "I have so much to do that I shall spend the first three hours in prayer."[4]

Studies have shown that the most successful people have a morning routine. Along with having a vision and clear goals, most high achievers have consistent early morning personal care regimens that go beyond breakfast and a shower. The healthiest and wealthiest people make the most of those early hours by planning, reading, studying, exercising, meditating and/or praying, and eating a nutritious breakfast. They nourish their bodies, minds, and souls. What begins well is more likely to end well. In fact, I believe that your physical, intellectual, and spiritual fitness is determined by how you steward those early hours of each day.

A successful morning routine begins with a successful evening routine. To start strong, you must end strong. I host the End Your Year Strong Empowerment Summit[5] each year so people will be in position to start the next year strong and empowered.

You have to set the stage for success. That means properly winding down at night so you can properly wind up in the morning. Turn off the screens, the television, the phone, and all your devices so you can set yourself up to prosper by reading a book, planning out the next day, setting out your workout clothes, tidying up, or whatever prepares you to begin the day empowered and strong. This will enable you to clear your mind so you can get a good night's rest. Those "me moments," as I call them, are for recharging your batteries, priming the pump, or winding up the top so you can be a force the next day that takes the world by storm.

Learn the art of commanding your morning. Through prayer and declarations of faith the night before, you can download success, progress, and prosperity into your tomorrow. Use your vision in praying and asking God for a specific strategy to bring it to pass.

Whether a person is brilliant and wealthy or uneducated and socioeconomically deprived, each is given the same twenty-four hours in a day. How you cultivate your time will determine the degree to which you are able to take advantage of any given opportunity.

As I explained in a previous chapter, although you can't actually "manage" time, you can manage yourself and your activities according to specific time frames. You can create an exceptional life by deliberately building into your daily routine specific objectives you wish to accomplish within specific frames of time that will bring you closer to fulfilling your purpose and maximizing your potential.

At the end of the day it all comes down to managing yourself.

You can decide what to do with the time you have been given. Attaining a quality life begins with a quality mindset about the precious commodity called time.

TELL YOUR TIME WHERE TO GO

Making the present a priority is essential to putting the past behind you. You must firmly plant yourself in the today you have been given to garner the forward momentum that will propel you into the future of your dreams. Leverage the present to move past the past. Saying hello to your tomorrow is the best way to say goodbye to your yesterday.[6] Think about what's next. Stir up your expectation for what you want to see happen. Create a little urgency for bringing those things to pass.

It is also helpful to learn to live in the tension between healthy anticipation and holy resting. The author of Hebrews wrote, "Let us labour therefore to enter into that rest" (Heb. 4:11). Another translation reads, "Let us therefore be diligent to enter that rest" (NKJV). It is interesting that we must *diligently labor* to enter His rest. This is like that creative tension you must hold between what is and what can be.

When you really understand the value of time, you will more actively take authority over it. You will recognize activities and people that waste your time, pulling away from those because they do not add value to your life. Consider who and what your time looters are. Do you have friends who are bored with their lives and want to waste time and money on consumptive activities and relationships? I have zero patience for people who mindlessly shop or just want to hang out. You've heard it said that you resemble those with whom you assemble. This speaks to the power of your relationships, but it also speaks to how you steward your time.

Don't just let life happen to you. Exercise the agency and "self-control" you have been given in Christ (2 Tim. 1:7, ESV) to take authority over your time. Remember, it's less about what you are demanding from life and more about what you are demanding from yourself. I've written an entire coaching module on how you can masterfully harness the power of time.[7] Simple tools from blocking or batching or identifying when you're most creative and what tasks belong in your genius zone can really improve effectiveness. You can even leverage waiting times to your benefit. Your time belongs to you.

Put yourself in the driver's seat of your life, take it out of park, and give it some gas. You can steer your life by plugging in the coordinates and telling your time machine where to go. You are a time traveler, so decide where you want it to take you. You are in control of your destiny and can accomplish whatever you want once you learn how to discern the seasons and expertly ride the waves of any given day.

Don't allow time to get the best of you; get the best of it. Don't squander the time you've been given because how you choose to use it determines the quality of your life. If you devalue your time, you devalue your life. Make the most of your life by making the most of your time.

> This is the day the LORD has made; we will rejoice and be glad in it.
>
> —PSALM 118:24, NKJV

PART THREE

• • •

Reclaim

· · ·

CHAPTER 7

Be Purpose Driven

THE LAW OF ASSIGNMENT

And God made two great lights; the greater
light to rule the day, and the lesser light to rule
the night: he made the stars also....And the
evening and the morning were the fourth day.
—GENESIS 1:16, 19

IT IS THE fourth day of divine creativity. Our Creator God, following His modus operandi of speaking things into existence, has called forth the seas and the skies, the seasons, years, and rhythm of days. God created the sun and the moon, and each received a specific assignment. The sun was assigned to govern, rule, and dominate the day, while the moon was given the night to govern, rule, and dominate. God made the stars, sprinkled across the sky like millions of twinkling fireflies, and they had assignments too. Stars helped chart the beginnings and endings of seasons and serve as a universal navigation system.

Everything God created was designed to fulfill a specific assignment, and that assignment is always to bring Him glory.

> The heavens declare the glory of God; and the firmament shows His handiwork. Day unto day utters speech, and night unto night reveals knowledge. There is no speech nor language where their voice is not heard. Their line has gone out through all the earth, and their words to the end of the world. In them He has set a tabernacle for the sun, which is like a bridegroom coming out of his chamber, and rejoices like a strong man to run its race. Its rising is from one end of heaven, and its circuit to the other end; and there is nothing hidden from its heat.
> —Psalm 19:1–6, nkjv

As Christ Himself proclaimed, so should each of us be able to one day declare with Him, "I glorified You on the earth, having accomplished the work which You have given me to do" (John 17:4, nasb).

An assignment is a designated duty you are given to perform, a delegated task to discharge, an enterprise to execute, or an initiative to complete. Even as God created two great lights, each with a specific assignment to fulfill, so He has given you and every person born on the earth an assignment. You might be tempted to disqualify yourself from that realm of greatness if you compare yourself to those you see as having a special calling to do great things. But let me assure you, there is no inferior or insignificant assignment from God.

This story about a little girl and a few pennies proves that.[1]

One Sunday pastor Russell H. Conwell found children

waiting outside the Sunday school room because it was too crowded for them to get in. One little girl, Hattie May Wiatt, lived nearby and, holding onto her books and her contribution, was trying to decide whether to wait or go home. Pastor Conwell picked her up, put her on his shoulders, and carried her into the classroom, finding a chair for her in the back.

The next day the pastor met her walking to school and told her that they would have a larger Sunday school room soon. She said that she hoped so because it was so crowded, she was afraid to go there alone. He assured her that they would begin raising money soon to build a new school building with enough room for all the children to attend. Pastor Conwell admitted that this was more of a vision than a reality, but he wanted to engage in conversation with Hattie.

Soon Hattie became sick, and though Pastor Conwell prayed for her, she died. At the funeral, Hattie's mother handed the pastor a little bag with fifty-seven cents in it that Hattie had been saving toward the larger Sunday school room.

Pastor Conwell took the money to church and announced that they had the first contribution toward the new school building. He exchanged the coins for fifty-seven pennies and auctioned them off, bringing in $250. With this money, they bought a house next to the church to enlarge the Sunday school. Plus, fifty-four of the fifty-seven cents were donated back to the church.

Soon that was not large enough, so they approached a nearby landowner about purchasing his lot. When he heard about the story, he reduced his price and took the fifty-four cents as a down payment.

Eventually, this small donation led to the founding of Temple University and Samaritan Hospital (now Temple University Hospital) as well as the enlarging of the church. Pastor Conwell hung a portrait of Hattie in his office to remind him of this remarkable story.

Sometimes we are stymied by our own small thinking about what God is able to do with the seemingly inconsequential thing we have been given to do or with the puny resources at our disposal. Consider what would have happened if that little girl had thought there was nothing she could do and hadn't put those few coins aside. What seemed like a worthless amount of loose change was able to recharge and revitalize an entire community. With this motivation, they were able to build a hospital, a university, a church, and yes, more facilities for children's Sunday school classes. One small girl's simple contribution changed the city, made history, and created exponential eternal impact. This story teaches us that whatever small thing we have been assigned to do has the power to change the world.

The secret to living a successful life, of making the most of your time on earth, includes harnessing the power of assignment. As you learn to let go of yesterday and embrace the freshness of God's power and provision for each new day, embrace the power of your assignment.

PREDESTINED FOR SUCCESS

Everything about you is well planned, divinely premeditated, sovereignly prearranged, and consciously thought out. God will quite literally move heaven and earth for you to successfully perform and complete your assignment. In his letter to the Romans, Paul wrote:

> For whom he did foreknow, he also did predestinate to be conformed to the image of his Son, that he might be the firstborn among many brethren. Moreover whom he did predestinate, them he also called: and whom he called, them he also justified: and whom he justified, them he also glorified. What shall we then say to these things? If God be for us, who can be against us?
>
> —ROMANS 8:29–31

The word *predestinate* comes from the Greek *proorizo*. It was formed from *pro*, meaning "before,"[2] and *horizo*, meaning "to mark out or bound ('horizon')."[3] Together they refer to something that stretches out before you. *Predestinate* also means "to foreordain, appoint beforehand; of God decreeing from eternity."[4] Before you were formed in your mother's womb, God put in place everything you would need to fulfill His purpose for your life. He determined your height, stature, and physique. He selected your gifts, talents, and abilities, and designed you to successfully complete what you've been given to do. Since purpose is the reason for your existence, you are purpose-built to fulfill your assignment.

The words of Psalm 139 can boost your understanding of God's thoughts toward you, especially when you feel unsure, insignificant, and out of place. I want to lead you through this passage phrase by phrase, excavating revelation that will give you confidence to embrace your assignment. Take a moment to meditate on this passage of Scripture.

> I will praise You, for I am fearfully and wonderfully made; marvelous are Your works, and that my soul knows very well. My frame was not hidden from You, when I was made in secret, and skillfully wrought in the lowest parts of the earth. Your eyes saw my substance, being yet unformed. And in Your book they all were written, the days fashioned for me, when as yet there were none of them. How precious also are Your thoughts to me, O God! How great is the sum of them! If I should count them, they would be more in number than the sand; when I awake, I am still with You.
>
> —PSALM 139:14–18, NKJV

David declared, "I will praise You, for I am fearfully and wonderfully made." The words translated "fearfully and wonderfully made" come from the Hebrew word *palah*, which means "to be distinct, be separated, be distinguished."[5] The next phrase we read is that God's works are *marvelous*, which is also the Hebrew word *pala'*, and it means "to be wonderful, be extraordinary."[6] That's you—God did wonderfully make *you*!

According to Psalm 139, God has written the story of your life—beginning, middle, and end. He knows all the plot twists, the climaxes, and the setups for the next scenes. He saw you in your imperfection and still embraced you and gave you purpose, which is not to be hidden away. Paul wrote to the Corinthians, "Ye are our epistle written in our hearts, known and read of all men" (2 Cor. 3:2). Our lives are to be lived out front and out loud so that we can be "known and read by all," to the praise and glory of God.

This is why David then declared in Psalm 139, "How precious

also are Your thoughts to me, O God! How great is the sum of them! If I should count them, they would be more in number than the sand" (vv. 17–18, NKJV). God has intricately woven together all the parts that make up the sum of who you are. You are marvelous and extraordinary. You are marked with distinction, uniqueness, worth, and dignity despite your imperfections. From the womb, you were already more than enough, one of a kind, unique, and set apart. You are built to be great and to live out an extraordinary purpose.

Once you understand your assignment, you will realize you have no competition. The sun and moon do not compete. They are both needed to complete the cycle of a day. Each is considered great and mysterious without the need to compete with the other. Likewise, you do not have to compete with anyone in this world because you are extraordinary in and of yourself. Understanding your assignment and fulfilling it is tapping into your greatness.

Declare this aloud now:

> *My relationships shall exist without strife or competition. I complement everyone around me, and everyone complements me. No one will strive with me. We operate by the law of increase and decrease.*

> *I am happy with my divine assignment. I refuse to compete with anyone. I am not jealous, envious, or angry. I am happy God made me exactly as I am.*

> *I am the light of the world, a city on a hill (Matt. 5:14). Therefore, I will let my light shine before people*

> *so they will see my good works and glorify my Father*
> *in heaven (v. 16).*
>
> *God has established me in this world to advance His*
> *kingdom. Nothing I do is insignificant, no matter*
> *how small the task or miniscule the assignment.*
>
> *I shall understand and comply with the divine pro-*
> *tocol for my life. I shall fulfill my purpose, maximize*
> *my potential, and accomplish my daily assignments. I*
> *shall rule as a thought leader within all my spheres of*
> *influence.*

Everything in the universe has an assignment. Pray daily
for yours.

THE FOURTH DAY

On the fourth day God put the finishing touches on the
environment of the earth and the sky that He made for man.
(See Genesis 1:19.) The number four is significant in understanding the order and structure of your assignment. The
Bible describes the four corners of the earth (Isa. 11:12) and
the four rivers that flow from Eden (Gen. 2:10–14).[7] There
are four main phases of the moon: the new moon, the first
quarter, the full moon, and the last quarter.[8] We experience
four seasons: spring, summer, autumn, and winter. Even our
days are divided into four parts: morning, noon, evening,
and night.

As you become aware of the specifics of your assignment,
you will come alive in your own spiritual fourth day when

96

the elements of your assignment begin to take shape. You will awaken to the significance of the purpose for which you have been built. Your directions, cycles, times, and seasons will align and give you focus and determination to live each moment with greater intention and deliberation. Your fourth day is your coming of age, the day it becomes clear that when you live fully aware of your assignment, you will prosper.

I want to challenge you to take time every four days to reconsider the assignment you've been given. Pray that God will help you carry out your part of manifesting His will on earth as it is in heaven. What you need going forward are the principles of the Law of Assignment to give you the parameters within which you will thrive.

THE LAW OF ASSIGNMENT

Soon after God established the earth and all that is in it, He made man and woman. Then He blessed them and gave them their first assignments.

> And God blessed them, and God said unto them, Be fruitful, and multiply, and replenish the earth, and subdue it: and have dominion over the fish of the sea, and over the fowl of the air, and over every living thing that moveth upon the earth.
>
> —GENESIS 1:28

Adam and Eve's assignments linger in the genetic memory of all humans who have ever lived. Each of us has a part in maintaining and moving forward the sevenfold creation mandate.

97

1. Be fruitful.

2. Multiply.

3. Replenish.

4. Subdue.

5. Have dominion (lead well within your realm or region of influence).

6. Live healthily (mind, body, and spirit).

7. Be productive.

Before God gives an assignment, He blesses the ones to whom He is assigning the task. His blessing is a necessary prerequisite to fulfilling purpose successfully. In his letter to Timothy, Paul wrote that we have been called "according to His own purpose and grace which was given to us in Christ Jesus before time began" (2 Tim. 1:9, NKJV). Purpose is the assignment you have been given, and grace is the power to fulfill it. God confers upon us His grace and favor, the two supernatural forces that empower you to prosper in your assignment (Deut. 15:10).

Furthermore, God's blessing commands resources to manifest as needed in order for you to prosper in the mission you've been sent to accomplish. His blessing pronounces abundant success over all our efforts.

Within this atmosphere are principles you must understand and work in tandem with so you will complete projects, strategies, operations, and collaborations. Here are fourteen principles that undergird the Law of Assignment.

1. Everything in the universe has an assignment.

God delegated certain responsibilities to each system in the universe. The sun regulates the daily cycles. The moon affects tides. If they do not fulfill their assignments, there will not be any seasons, signs, hours, days, or years. It is imperative that everything fulfills its assignments as it complements everything else.

2. Every person on the earth has an assignment.

From the beginning God assigned Adam and Eve to rule, be fruitful, and multiply. Noah was assigned to build the ark. Moses was assigned to affect the social systems and institutions as a great deliverer of the Hebrew nation.

From Old Testament to the New Testament, from the age of the prophets, judges, and kings to the era of the disciples, the church, and its leaders, we see the vivid picture of the power of assignment activated on page after page of miraculous accounts. Paul made clear in his letter to the Colossians, "I, Paul, have been sent on a special assignment by Christ as part of God's master plan" (Col. 1:1, MSG).

At the time, however, the main characters of these accounts may not have felt what they were doing was extraordinary. They were simply being obedient. The day-in, day-out grind was certainly never glamorous. They were often not recognized for accomplishing the divine assignments they were tasked with as "part of God's master plan." Yet, ordinary men and women were driven by something greater than themselves to faithfully use their everyday passions and propensities to make the world a better place. Just like them, you have an assignment that is "part of God's master plan." How you discharge your assignment will not only affect your destiny, but it will also affect the destinies of so many others.

3. Assignments are geo-specific.

There is a prophetic grid (a zip code) for where you are to fulfill your assignment. This place will have a magnetic pull on you based on your DNA, your purpose, and your mindset.

Adam fulfilled his assignment in the Garden of Eden. Moses fulfilled his assignment in Egypt and later in the wilderness. Daniel fulfilled his assignment in Babylon. John the Revelator fulfilled his on the isle of Patmos where he wrote the Book of Revelation. Winston Churchill's assignment was to England, and Barack Obama's was to the United States of America.

Perhaps you will be assigned, as I have, to various geographic locations for various times and purposes. I was born on a little island called Bermuda, then relocated to the United States. Yet I fulfill my assignments in different parts of the world: Nigeria, the Netherlands, Canada, Brazil, Bahamas, Jamaica, England, Guyana, South Africa, India, and more. God told Jeremiah, "I have this day set thee over the nations and over the kingdoms, to root out, and to pull down, and to destroy, and to throw down, to build, and to plant" (Jer. 1:10).

4. Assignments are time-specific.

Ecclesiastes 3:1 says, "To every thing there is a season, and a time to every purpose under the heaven." Don't be so caught up in your past that you don't take full advantage of the present.

Failure to fulfill a given assignment at the appointed time will have a potentially negative affect on your life. Ask God to give you insight into how to manage your activities according to specific time frames. Pray that the Lord will teach you to number your days, as Moses said in Psalm 90, so that you may apply wisdom to your heart (v. 12).

5. You must choose to fulfill your assignment.

"Many are called, but few are chosen" (Matt. 22:14). Why? Because the chosen do the choosing! You must choose to do what God has called you to do. How will you answer when the Lord says, "Your mission, should you choose to accept it, is...."?

Isaiah was caught up in a glorious heavenly scene. Angels were dispatched to ready him for what God was about to request. Everything in heaven and on the earth had been summoned and was at his disposal. The only thing left for Isaiah was to accept or reject the assignment. "I heard the voice of the Lord, saying, Whom shall I send, and who will go for us? Then said I, Here am I; send me" (Isa. 6:8).

Use your imagination to envision such a scene in the heavenlies whenever a child of God receives a new mission. All the cosmic materials and mysteries of the universe in heaven above and the earth beneath are at your disposal. You are qualified by purification and divine blessing to the mission you are tasked to do. However, it is your decision to say very simply, "Here am I; send me."

6. Assignments are success-oriented.

God does not give you an assignment to fail. He guarantees success, as He defines it, for every assignment He gives you. Success is the sum of small efforts done repeatedly day in and day out. Success is not a single major accomplishment but the sum total of many actions taken and wise decisions made consistently over time, which is what we call a habit. As stated by United Kingdom's former Prime Minister Benjamin Disraeli, "The secret of success is constancy of purpose."[9] Determination today leads to success tomorrow.

> This book of the law shall not depart out of thy mouth; but thou shalt meditate therein day and night, that thou mayest observe to do according to all that is written therein: for then thou shalt make thy way prosperous, and then thou shalt have good success.
>
> —Joshua 1:8

7. Assignments are others-focused.

Have you heard of the idea that the flapping of a butterfly's wings in California affects the wind current in Calcutta? In this manner your life assignment has an impact on the world at large. Fulfilling it makes you a significant contributor to the unfolding of God's plan for humanity.

During the Vietnam War, US Navy pilot Charles Plumb's jet was hit by a surface-to-air missile. Plumb ejected in time, parachuted to the ground and was captured. For almost six years he was a prisoner of war.

Years after he returned home, Plumb and his wife were eating in a restaurant. A man at another table recognized him as the pilot who was on the aircraft carrier Kitty Hawk and who was shot down. He even remembered Plumb's name.

Plumb asked him how he knew it was him.

The man answered, "I packed your parachute."

Plumb was shocked and overcome with gratitude. The man shook his hand and noted, "I guess it worked!" Plumb assured him that it had, or he wouldn't have been there talking with him.

That night Plumb lay awake thinking about that man. He tried to recall what he might have looked like in his Navy uniform and wondered if he had seen him on the carrier. In fact, Plumb wondered if he ever greeted him or asked him how he was, remembering the prideful distance between a fighter pilot and a sailor.

As Plumb reflected on the hours the sailor had spent in the heart of the ship, carefully folding each parachute, he thought about how that sailor held in his hands the lives of all those pilots he never knew.[10]

Who's packing your parachute? Or whose parachute are you packing? Every successful person has someone working behind the scenes, providing what they need to make it through the day. This is the power of relationship. Who in your life is taking care to make sure you have a properly packed parachute? And how are you using your life to help others?

8. Assignments require fortitude.

In her 2014 best-selling book, *13 Things Mentally Strong People Don't Do*, Amy Morin outlines behaviors that you should *not* practice if you want to "take back your own power, embrace change, face your fears, and train your brain for happiness and success."[11] These traits are essential to developing the grit it takes to see your assignment through to completion.[12] Amy makes these points about mentally strong people:

- They don't waste time feeling sorry for themselves.

- They don't give away their power.

- They don't shy away from change.

- They don't focus on things they can't control.

- They don't worry about pleasing everyone.

- They don't fear taking calculated risks.

- They don't dwell on the past.

- They don't make the same mistakes over and over.

- They don't resent other people's success.

- They don't give up after the first failure.

- They don't fear alone time.

- They don't feel the world owes them anything.

- They don't expect immediate results.

As the Scriptures say, you may plant or you may water, but then trust God with the increase (1 Cor. 3:6–9).

Morin says that mental strength is about "improving your ability to regulate your emotions, manage your thoughts, and behave in a positive manner, despite your circumstances."[13] In order to do this well, Morin says you must 1) recognize irrational thoughts and substitute realistic thoughts; 2) act positively in spite of the situation; and 3) exert control over your feelings so they don't control you.[14] Mental toughness and fortitude are essential keys to success.

You cannot afford to give up when things go wrong. You must fortify your mind. Remember, the enemy mentally attacked Jesus when He was led into the wilderness for forty days (Matt. 4:1–11), and he will attack you too. But Jesus overcame, and so can you because you have the mind of Christ: "Let this mind be in you, which was also in Christ Jesus" (Phil. 2:5).

9. Assignments require focus.

If you care about what other people think about you, you will become a slave to their thoughts and expectations. But if you care about what God thinks about you, you will be liberated to fulfill purpose, maximize potential, and succeed in the process! Heed the words of the apostle Peter who counseled, "Wherefore gird up the loins of your mind, be sober, and hope to the end for the grace that is to be brought unto you at the revelation of Jesus" (1 Pet. 1:13). Focus on what God says about who you are and what He has for you: "For I know the thoughts that I think toward you, says the LORD, thoughts of peace and not of evil, to give you a future and a hope" (Jer. 29:11, NKJV).

10. Assignments require commitment.

Everyone is committed to something, even if only half committed. But 50 percent commitment is not the same as 100 percent commitment. You must be all in.

Once you know your mission, you must break commitments with everything else that does not lead to fulfilling your assignment, so you focus all your energy on the main thing. Don't tire yourself out on fruitless activities only to discover that when it comes time to do your assignment, you are spent or burned out. Instead, you must be steadfast, faithful, and diligent. Both your level of commitment and the task you are committing to do dictate the stamina you will have to keep going. Never give up until your assignment is complete.

11. Assignments require sensitivity to the Holy Spirit.

Look at the life of Paul, a man of such purpose and vision that he evangelized an entire region of the globe and wrote most of the New Testament—and that was before there were laptops or the internet, let alone vehicles. What was the key to his success besides fortitude, focus, and commitment? He was continually led by the Holy Spirit. "And a vision appeared to Paul in the night; There stood a man of Macedonia…saying, Come over into Macedonia, and help us. And after he had seen the vision, immediately we endeavored to go into Macedonia" (Acts 16:9–10).

We also read in Paul's first letter to the Corinthians that he instructed, "Only, as the Lord has assigned to each one, as God has called each, in this manner let him walk" (1 Cor. 7:17, NASB).

12. Assignments require faith.

Faith is the foundation of your relationship with God. Without trusting Him with your life, you will not have the drive to believe His Word regarding His call on your life. You will not trust Him with the outcome. Therefore, you will have no real reason to do as He leads. You will not wholeheartedly believe in who the Bible says He is. God's omnipotence, omnipresence, and omniscience will be challenged by your distrust. Instead, you must believe that His thoughts and ways are higher than yours (Isa. 55:9), that He knows the beginning from the end (Isa. 46:10), and that His lovingkindness toward you is everlasting (Ps. 136).

Trust is also the precedent to pleasing God and invoking His favor and grace on your life. It is the driving factor to being able to submit to Him for the correction and guidance you need to successfully complete your assignment. "Trust in the LORD with all your heart, and lean not on your own understanding; in all your ways acknowledge Him, and He shall direct your paths" (Prov. 3:5–6, NKJV).

13. Your assignments are interrelated with others' assignments.

Throughout the Bible we see that one person's assignment was woven together with another person's assignment. Ruth was a maidservant, an immigrant who worked part-time for Boaz. As she discharged her daily assignment, she caught Boaz's attention. She eventually married Boaz, and they both became the ancestors of two of ancient Israel's most powerful kings, Saul and David, as well as our Savior Jesus Christ.

Sarah's assignment was interrelated with Abraham's. Jonathan, although son of King Saul, was assigned to David, his father's successor. Rahab's assignment enabled Israel's spies to fulfill their assignments.

From these examples we can see how "the whole body, joined and knit together by what every joint supplies, according to the effective working by which every part does its share, causes growth of the body for the edifying of itself in love" (Eph. 4:16, NKJV).

14. Assignments are problem-oriented.

As it has often been said, "The significant problems we have cannot be solved at the same level of thinking with which we created them." It is easy for us to look at the magnitude of world problems and wait for someone else to find the solution. As overwhelming as many of them are, in the words of Marie Curie, "Nothing in life needs to be feared, it is only to be understood."[15] We just have to pray and ponder about a problem long enough for God to reveal the solution, for, as it has been said, "No problem can stand the assault of sustained thinking."

It is easy for us to look at the magnitude of world problems and wait for someone else to find the solution. As overwhelming as many of these problems are, you just have to pray and ponder a problem long enough for God to reveal the solution—or at least, your part in the solution.

You are given an assignment because there is a problem. Esther's nation was threatened with ethnic cleansing, and God selected her to solve it. You are a problem solver. If you examine the Bible, you will discover that all great leaders solved problems. Joseph solved Pharaoh's problem. Moses solved Israel's slavery problem. Gideon and David solved a terrorism problem. Jacob solved a corporate problem and took a startup company to the proverbial Fortune 500 status. Rahab solved the spies' problem. Jesus solved the sin problem.

You are needed to solve a problem. When there are no problems, you cease to be needed. The problem gives you a purpose and the assignment needed to solve it. Without the problem, you cease to walk in the favor and grace God gives you to pursue it.

> The lines of purpose in your lives never grow slack, tightly tied as they are to your future in heaven, kept taut by hope.... We pray that you'll live well for the Master, making Him proud of you as you work hard in His orchard. As you learn more and more how God works, you will learn how to do your work. We pray that you'll have the strength to stick it out over the long haul—not the grim strength of gritting your teeth but the glory-strength God gives. It is strength that endures the unendurable and spills over into joy, thanking the Father who makes us strong enough to take part in everything bright and beautiful that he has for us.
> —COLOSSIANS 1:5, 10–12, MSG

CHAPTER 8

Practice the Art of Abundance

THE LAW OF ABUNDANCE

And God said, Let the waters bring forth
abundantly the moving creature that hath
life, and fowl that may fly above the earth
in the open firmament of heaven. And God
created great whales, and every living creature
that moveth, which the waters brought forth
abundantly, after their kind, and every winged
fowl after his kind: and God saw that it was
good. And God blessed them, saying, Be
fruitful, and multiply, and fill the waters in the
seas, and let fowl multiply in the earth. And the
evening and the morning were the fifth day.
—GENESIS 1:20–23

THE GENESIS ACCOUNT of creation reveals that before God made each creature, He created a sustaining environment in which that creature could thrive and survive. Each was an abundant environment, prepared with care for those who would live in it.

On the first day God created light, and on the fourth day He created light-givers in the form of the sun and the moon to disperse the light and regulate day and night. On day two He created the waters below and the skies above. Then on day five He populated the waters with sea creatures and the skies with birds of every kind. The dry land and its vegetation were created on the third day, and on day six God populated it with animals and human life, placing these living creatures in an environment already prepared with fruits, vegetables, and plants.

All these plants were seed bearing so they could reproduce after their own kind. God sustains what He creates. What does this mean for you? It means that you never have to worry about whether you will have sufficient resources. You serve a God who is the keeper of what He creates and who specializes in abundance.

The first chapter of Genesis is replete with acts of a God rich in supply. For all who would understand God not only as Creator but also as Provider and Sustainer, it is essential to meditate on this first chapter of Genesis. You serve a God who delights to supply all your needs in Christ Jesus (Phil. 4:19).

> Why take ye thought for raiment? Consider the lilies of the field, how they grow; they toil not, neither do they spin: and yet I say unto you, that even Solomon in all

his glory was not arrayed like one of these. Wherefore, if God so clothed the grass of the field, which to day is, and to morrow is cast into the oven, shall he not much more clothe you, O ye of little faith? Therefore take no thought, saying, What shall we eat? or, What shall we drink? or, Wherewithal shall we be clothed? (For after all these things do the Gentiles seek:) for your heavenly Father knoweth that ye have need of all these things.

—MATTHEW 6:28–32

In his book *Thou Shall Prosper*, Rabbi Daniel Lapin shares the significance of the Jewish *Havdalah* service that is recited on Saturday evening as the Sabbath wanes and families get ready to begin the new week. *Havdalah* commemorates the separation of the divine and the mundane and the Sabbath from the workweek, but also emphasizes the importance of remembering the holiness of the Sabbath during the other six days of the week.[1]

As Rabbi Lapin points out, *Havdalah* highlights the hands, asking for blessing on whatever work, assignment, or duty those hands are used to perform. *Havdalah* is recited over a cup into which wine is poured until it overflows into its saucer. A prayer is spoken which asks God to increase the family's offspring and wealth.

According to Rabbi Lapin, first your own cup is filled. The overflow symbolizes having sufficient to motivate others. As Rabbi Lapin explains it:

> This overflowing cup symbolizes the intention to produce during the week ahead not only sufficient to fill one's cup,

but also an excess that will allow overflow for the benefit of others. In other words, I am obliged to first full my cup and then continue pouring as it were, so that I will have sufficient to give away to others, thus helping to jump-start their own efforts. Judaism views attending to your own vineyard not as shameful, but as a moral obligation.[2]

The concept of living with overflow is important because this abundance can only come from an acknowledgement of our ability to produce more than we need. Abundance is accessible to all. Don't miss recognizing that abundance is all around us and that we have the ability to fully engage with it.

The most common narrative today equates having more than enough with being selfish. Along with that flows an undercurrent of frustration about having to give out of lack. This comes from a scarcity mentality that believes there is only so much and no more. This mentality confuses the limitations of the finite world with the abundance of possibilities available through the infinite, eternal kingdom of God.

Modern culture and the media convey the message that certain resources are limited: We only have so much more oil, so much more air, so much more money we can earn. The rich may enjoy luxuries, but there is not enough for the rest of us. This thinking implies that there is only so much wealth in the world, which is why the 99 percent must stand up against the 1 percent and demand they give back their share by paying higher taxes and funding programs to help all those who cannot help themselves.

In hearing this again and again, we have accepted the

subconscious message that we are playing a zero-sum game: that for every fraction more of the pie one person gets, someone else must receive a fraction less. This mentality believes that the more wealth one person amasses, the less there is for everyone else. With this mindset, Bill Gates could be seen as being directly responsible for the growing problem of poverty in the world. If he would only give up more of his billions, people in developing countries would be less likely to starve to death. Yet Bill and Melinda Gates have given generously through the Bill & Melinda Gates Foundation, and the poor still starve. Clearly billionaires giving away billions is not the answer.

Governments, NGOs, and wealthy individuals have been pouring money into poverty and hunger issues for decades. If more money were the solution, we wouldn't still have world hunger. The problem isn't a lack of money; it's something else. This is why the foundation Bill Gates started is actively involved in finding alternative ways to address pressing problems in the world that money alone cannot solve. The Trimm International Foundation is doing that as well.[3]

REJECT THE ZERO-SUM MENTALITY

Zero-sum thinking assumes we have limited options, that we have to forfeit something like time, money, or effort in exchange for what we need. When we give up, we lose, and someone else benefits. Everything is basically a lose-win proposition. But this is not so. God has built abundance and wealth into the DNA of His creation.

Let me give you an example. Let's say you need groceries, but the closest store to your house is more expensive than you like. You could complain and pay the prices or drive farther away to shop elsewhere. However, if those are the only two options you believe you have, you are engaging in zero-sum thinking. The truth is that you have far more than two options, but you have to engage your imagination to figure out what they are. That's the line most people never attempt to cross.

Crossing that line might mean ordering your groceries from an online wholesaler and having them delivered. Or you might choose to eat less or simplify your diet. Perhaps an option could be finding a plot of land on which to grow your own vegetables. If you were really enterprising, you could open your own store. You are only limited by your lack of imagination.

In such situations, however, most people choose to complain rather than to create. They don't see their options because they have accepted the zero-sum thinking that society preaches to them. Of course, in order to understand this, you must learn to think creatively, to think outside the box. You have to think like a person of overflow rather than a person of barely enough.

The real world is not nearly as limited as most of us assume. When one person in a community makes money, we think someone else must have gotten poorer. But that's not really what happens. Instead, the spender gets a benefit while the seller receives money to use to get a benefit from someone else. As someone gains more money, that person has more money to spend. Even basic transactions are not zero-sum exchanges because money is exchanged for something of value. People get more money because they give more value. Spending money is a value exchange.

If you buy a refrigerator at a local appliance store so your food stays fresh longer and you throw less of it away, you save money in the long run. The refrigerator merchant makes money and uses it to stay in operation, creating jobs that enable people to pay for the goods and services others provide that benefit the community, including you. That merchant also pays taxes (as do you) so the streets get repaired, the police and firefighters get better equipped, and numerous other public services are provided. Each transaction is an exchange of value.

Develop an abundance mentality that says your cup overflows (Ps. 23:5). Think about this. When someone spends five dollars at a local merchant, has the local economy only increased by five dollars? No! Because of the indirect and induced impact of the money spent, the effect on the local economy is greater than the direct impact of that five dollars.[4]

How does this happen? The initial merchant made five dollars, then spent it at the local coffee shop, whose owner buys coffee beans from a local wholesaler, who spends that money for groceries. The grocer then uses the gain as part of paying his landlord, who buys flowers for his wife at the local florist. If that same five dollars is exchanged merely ten times within the community, it creates fifty dollars in value. If that five-dollar bill were exchanged one hundred times, then it would create five hundred dollars in value for the community. That is why, when the economy is bad, governments do what they can to increase people's spending. The more that money changes hands, the more a community prospers. Commerce makes economies hum.

Though the difference in net worth between the merchant and his neighbors may grow a little wider, everyone in the community has more money than they did before and has a better standard of living because the merchant's business is successful.

Of course, people can be greedy, local officials can abuse their power, and merchants can charge too much for their goods or services. Those in power who have more money can take advantage of those who have less. But that is because of the ethics, selfishness, foolishness, and lack of self-leadership of those suffering from a zero-sum mindset, not the amount of money in play.

Money is a type of currency, not the type of conductor. Money is simply a means to an end, not the end itself. It is a tool used to exchange value or create value. The issue that keeps us from our dreams is not how much money we have, but instead how much wealth we can create. The more wealth and value we create, the more others will exchange their dollar bills to get it. The issue is seldom money, but rather our ability to create wealth.

Zero-sum thinking reveals the fundamental misconception that money and wealth are the same thing; that the more money you have, the wealthier you are. The full truth is that the wealthier you are, the less money you need, though the more of it you are likely to attract. To master the art of abundance, you must opt out of the zero-sum game by garnering an accurate understanding of true wealth.

TRUE WEALTH

While there is a correlation between how much money you have and how much wealth you have, the opposite is *not* true:

the less money you have, the less wealthy you are. Wealth and money are different. Money is a physical representation of value, a means of exchange to simplify commerce so we don't have to trade rutabagas or goats for goods and services! Wealth, on the other hand, is spiritual and ethereal. At its core, wealth is simply *ability*. Wealth comes from the internal, spiritual realm; money is exterior and physical. Money can represent wealth, but it is not what wealth truly is.

As the saying goes, "Money can't buy you love." But the wealth of one's soul connecting with the wealth of another makes love possible. All the money in the world can't buy you a happy, healthy family. But what you put into your family and create together is one of the deepest kinds of wealth that exists on our planet. Money doesn't provide medical expertise, but the wealth of the doctors' experience and their ability to apply their wealth of medical wisdom can bring healing to patients.

Do you have a problem you need to solve? Money can hire someone to help you solve it, but the wealth of knowledge that person carries is what actually solves the problem. If the person you hired had faced your problem, no money would be needed because that person could just have applied his or her wealth of wisdom, ability, and experience to solve it.

Wealth means that whatever you want to do, you can do it. If you have some money, you can usually find a way to turn it into wealth, to turn it into knowledge, expertise, or experience that will give you the ability to exchange value for what you want to do or create. The mind is what contains and creates wealth. You can either use your own mind, which is free, or hire someone else's. Or you can create mutually beneficial relationships in which wealth-creating ideas are exchanged. In fact, true wealth is usually produced in relationships created through teamwork, friendship, or kinship. Businesses often think of themselves as families because good relationships multiply wealth.

I have heard it said that the only real difference between a rich person, a middle-class person, and a poor person is the way each perceives the world around them. Like an elephant convinced that a piece of string can tether its leg to a peg in the ground, you may be conditioned by external forces to believe you will never escape the way you are living. Poor people who think like poor people tend to stay poor. Poor people who learn to think like rich people tend to become rich. Though it may not be an easy process, it is just that simple. The answer is not more money; it's using your mind to cultivate more wealth. God gives you the power to create wealth (Deut. 8:18).

If you want to be rich, you must figure out how to recognize and leverage the wealth you have or how to gain additional wealth through learning and developing new skills. God is not against your being rich or wealthy. In fact, Paul instructs his ministerial protégé Timothy about this.

> Charge them that are rich in this world, that they be not highminded, nor trust in uncertain riches, but in the living God, who giveth us richly all things to enjoy; that they do good, that they be rich in good works, ready to distribute, willing to communicate; laying up in store for

themselves a good foundation against the time to come,
that they may lay hold on eternal life.

—1 Timothy 6:17–19

Money in the bank is wonderful and having it gives you options. But if you know how to harness the power of the wealth you have, to increase your own personal capacity to create value, you will become a light in the world of darkness and an instrument in the hand of God to make this world a better place.

The bottom line is that most of us are much wealthier than we think, and we have the potential to create much more wealth than we ever imagined. If you had more, you could do more. But don't make the pursuit of wealth a greater priority than the pursuit of the kingdom because that is where the true treasure lies.

Seek ye first the kingdom of God, and his righteousness; and all these things shall be added unto you.

—Matthew 6:33

THE LAW OF ABUNDANCE

You must recognize that you are inherently wealthy and that you live in an abundant world if you are going to help others. Two drowning people can't help each other unless one of them is holding onto something stable. Two people walking through the desert with only enough water for one are not both going to make it to the other side. Only the person with enough for herself plus enough for the other will have a chance of leading both to safety.

Who is going to listen to a poor person speak about how to get out of poverty? It's hard to lift someone out of a ditch until you have climbed out yourself. The only other way to get out is for one person to step on top of another, but then neither are better off. Believing that becoming a doormat is being a servant leader is not of service to anyone. You must model the self-mastery you want to see in others. To become an example, you must change yourself first.

If you aren't motivated to live abundantly by building the wealth of your own personal capacity for your own good, then do it for those you love or out of service for others. Lee Kuan Yew, Singapore's talented prime minister from 1959 to 1990, described this principle as a key component in helping him take Singapore from a third-world island dependent on its British colonizers to one of the most vibrant first-world economies.

> There is a little Chinese aphorism which encapsulates this idea: *Xiushen qijia zhiguo pingtianxia*. *Xiushen* means look after yourself, cultivate yourself, do everything to make yourself useful; *Qijia*, look after the family; *Zhiguo*, look after your country; *Pingtianxia*, all is peaceful under heaven.... It is the basic concept of our civilization. Governments will come, governments will go, but this endures.[5]

You can only bring others into abundance when you have beaten a trail there yourself. You can only give greatly when you have a great deal to give.

In the West today we focus on individual rights and becoming the best each of us can be. However, we lose something very fundamental when we fail to recognize both our need for others and what we can contribute to the health of our communities as a whole. Our individual freedoms do not need to be at odds with our personal responsibilities to our communities. Demanding the right to enjoy life as we see fit results in failing to recognize the impact our indulgent "success" has on the lives of others. We pursue such "success" in order to consume, and then we complain that we don't have enough. Instead, we should work to fill our cups in order to have overflow to give to others. Then we will recognize that the world is full of limitless win-win possibilities, and we will raise the water level of abundance for all.

If you want to make a real impact on the world, you must do it from a place of responsibility, wholeness, and competence. Remember the lessons of *Havdalah*: Carry a mindset of abundant possibility with you in everything you set your hands to do. Recognize that only when you have more than you need can you help others plug into the abundance they need. Never stop improving yourself so that you have more and more to give. It is only then that you will make yourself truly rich and powerful, with the divine abundance that empowers you to leave your mark on history.

Declare abundance over your life. Declare no more lack or limitations but abundance and options. Declare that you have:

- abundant health

- abundant wealth

- abundant joy

- abundant peace
- abundant relationships
- abundant wisdom
- abundant love
- abundant faith

Boldly declare:

- A place has been made for me among the great and mighty.

- I declare abundance over my life, thoughts, ideas, home, family, spouse, children, work, ministry, business, projects, products, goods, and services.

- I declare abundance over my local schools, government, neighborhood, church, community, and nation.

- I thrive within an environment that is conducive to whom God made me to be and what He created me to achieve, accomplish, and become.

God abundantly filled the environments He created in the first chapter of Genesis. He put the Law of Abundance into motion so you also may bring forth abundantly, being fruitful and multiplying!

Now unto him that is able to do exceeding abundantly above all that we ask or think, according to the power that worketh in us, unto him be glory in the church by Christ Jesus throughout all ages, world without end. Amen.

—EPHESIANS 3:20–21

CHAPTER 9

Develop a Dominion Mindset

THE LAW OF GREATNESS

> Then God said, "Let Us make man in Our
> image, according to Our likeness; let them have
> dominion over...all the earth...." So God
> created man in His own image; in the image
> of God He created him; male and female He
> created them. Then God blessed them, and God
> said to them, "Be fruitful and multiply; fill the
> earth and subdue it; have dominion over the
> fish of the sea, over the birds of the air, and over
> every living thing that moves on the earth."
> —GENESIS 1:26–28, NKJV

"WE WILL REMEMBER that layup forever." Those were the words of the game announcer after nineteen-year-old Lauren Hill made her left-handed two-point basket for the Mount St. Joseph's home team in front of a sold-out crowd of ten thousand in Cincinnati's Xavier University Cintas Center.[1]

What college basketball player wouldn't be thrilled to feel the thunder of the floorboards, hear her name on the loud speaker, and see the people up on their feet, enthusiastically applauding her hard work and determination? It was a dream come true. The story is even more remarkable when you learn that it wasn't only the home team and their supporters who were cheering for Hill, but the entire stadium, including the referees and the opposing team.

Hill fell in love with basketball in the sixth grade, but shortly before she graduated from high school and headed off to fulfill her dream of playing collegiate ball, she was diagnosed with a rare type of terminal brain cancer. Her parents remember that she asked the doctor, "Can I at least still play basketball?"[2]

It wouldn't be easy, but then easy was never Hill's style. She had to learn to shoot with her left hand because the cancer had weakened her right side. She pushed aside her symptoms and still got up at 5:30 a.m. for basketball practice, even though she couldn't always do the drills.[3] She would do her part to be ready if she lived long enough to play NCAA ball.

Her life became very focused, living in the moment, and doing what she loved. "It's not something I've always done," she says. "It's almost like you've been sleeping your whole life, and someone says, 'Hey, wake up.'" Any spare time she had was devoted to serving those she loved. She confided, "I didn't know what [God] sent me here for. I wanted to know what He sent me here for." She told Him, "Whatever You sent me here for, I'm ready to do."[4] She became the voice for all the other children battling rare forms of cancer, giving interviews locally and nationally, and launching a nonprofit to raise research money.

The Hiram Terriers were the first opponents on the schedule and played a huge part in seeing Hill's dream come true. When they heard Hill's story, they suggested moving up the game two weeks and even offered to give up their home-court advantage so she could play in front of her family and friends. The NCAA made an exception to the rules and allowed for the adjustment in the schedule, and ten thousand tickets were sold—in an hour.[5]

Hill's team turned a rival into one big family by inviting the Terriers to dinner the night before the big game. The young women laughed, shared stories, and left with hugs all around. They were still competitors, but with more room in their hearts.

Those new connections showed up on the court too. When Hill hit that first shot, everything stopped as everyone shared in her glory. One of the Hiram Terriers revealed to a reporter that it was the "most happy feeling I've ever felt of an opponent scoring." When one of the Terriers later had a three-pointer swish through the net, she heard a Mount player say, "Great shot...glad you took it."[6]

Hill didn't have a fairy tale ending, though. Instead she had a new definition for a life fully lived that is not limited by number of days. Hill has left this world, but not without showing us that there is enough glory, fame, success, power, resources, and love to go around. You can make room for another life without diminishing your own. With a little determination, you don't have to allow any situation or circumstance limit what you are able to do with whatever time, energy, and resources God has given you. Your time on earth may not be limitless, but only you can limit what God can do through you.

Think about how you might impact the lives of others in the next few months. Perhaps that impact will be great enough to live beyond your allotted time on earth and influence future generations. Mount St. Joseph University President Tony Aretz said this of Hill in an interview:

> Her light will continue to shine on us all as her supporters worldwide continue her mission of increasing awareness and finding a cure for DIPG. We are forever grateful to have had Lauren grace our campus with her smile and determined spirit. She has left a powerful legacy. She taught us that every day is a blessing; every moment a gift.[7]

So many people live restricted lives for one reason or the other. They may suffer from debilitating illness or struggle to make ends meet. Some live in countries that prohibit freedom of speech or prohibit them from climbing the ladder of success because of gender, religion, or ethnicity. But when you know that your freedom is not based on external forces but comes from Jesus Christ, you will then understand that with God nothing is impossible.

Your greatness does not come from mere skill, talent, or ability, but it comes when you dare to live in the greatness of God. He is the one who has no limits and no boundaries. It is in Him that "we live, and move, and have our being" (Acts 17:28). We can trust He will complete the good work He has begun in us (Phil. 1:6) if we simply make room for His greatness to work through us.

> Trust in the LORD with all thine heart; and lean not
> unto thine own understanding. In all thy ways acknowl-
> edge him, and he shall direct thy paths.
>
> —PROVERBS 3:5–6

THE LAW OF GREATNESS

Life is full of challenges. I wish I could promise you that God will never lead you into hardship, but I can't. What I can promise you is that He will always be with you and that when you leave this life, you will be with Him eternally. Living forever in His glory indeed is limitless.

The essence of true life on this earth, too, is no limits because "He has planted eternity in the human heart" (Eccles. 3:11, NLT). He has placed us in Christ so that we "can do all things" (Phil. 4:13, NKJV) because "with God all things are possible" (Matt. 19:26, NKJV).

You have something great to do for God while you are here on this earth. You have His Spirit of greatness in your DNA. John tells us in his first epistle, "You are of God....He who is in you is greater than he who is in the world" (1 John 4:4, NKJV). When John says you are "of God," he means that you come from God. You were born of the greatness of God! His greatness is *in you*. Therefore, you are quite literally wired for greatness! You are greater than your circumstances and greater than any obstacle. Plus, according to this verse, God in you is greater than all the enemy's forces!

Don't underestimate the greatness that dwells in every fiber of your being. You are the carrier of mountain-moving faith (Mark 11:23), and you have the power of life and death in the words you speak (Prov. 18:21). You even have "power to tread on serpents and scorpions" and power "over all the power of the enemy" (Luke 10:19). "No weapon turned against you will succeed. You will silence every voice raised up to accuse you" (Isa. 54:17, NLT). You have limitless life in Christ. Don't sell yourself short by not living in the greatness He created you for in Him.

In Genesis 19 we read about the destruction of Sodom and Gomorrah and Lot's subsequent decision to settle in Zoar rather than head higher up into the mountains. The word *Tso`ar* (translated *Zoar*) means "insignificance."[8] Mountains speak of greatness. Why would anyone choose an insignificant life when God has something greater?

Lot settled in a place of insignificance out of fear. "Lot and his two daughters left Zoar and settled in the mountains, for he was afraid to [even] stay in Zoar. He and his two daughters lived in a cave" (Gen. 19:30, NIV). Although God sent angels to urge Lot to go to the mountains, Lot argued with God and refused to pursue His greater plan. He went up just far enough to avoid trouble, but then chose not to expend the energy to go any farther than the cave where he settled.

Never settle for less than God's best! Never allow fear of the unknown to force you into settling for less than the greatness God has for you. The opposite of greatness is not only insignificance, but also being average and mediocre. Settling for life of mediocrity means you refuse to believe in either your own greatness in Christ or in the greatness of God. The people we read about in the Bible were great because they trusted in God's greatness. They were mighty because they lived in the strength of God. They were wise because they lived in the wisdom of God. They were knowledgeable because they lived in the knowledge of God.

Maybe you feel that you don't deserve better, or maybe you simply refuse to challenge yourself. Instead you end up choosing to live in the comfort of the commonplace, not wanting to risk being misjudged, misunderstood, disappointed, or rejected. Some people have mistaken being average for being humble, believing that a lackluster existence is somehow honoring God. This is a tragic deception. A mindset that gives way to mediocrity fails to recognize that God created human beings in His image as representatives of His excellence and glory:

> In whom [Christ] also we have obtained an inheritance, being predestinated according to the purpose of Him who worketh all things after the counsel of his own will: that we should be to the praise of his glory.
> —Ephesians 1:11–12

Most people don't embrace the fullness of their potential for fear of being considered arrogant. Frankly, people are sometimes incorrectly called arrogant when they refuse to adjust to low expectations, refuse to accept the status quo, or refuse to let go of a grand vision they have for improving themselves and the world around them.

Remember, you serve a great God who created you for so much more when He created you in *His* image and after *His* likeness (Gen. 1:26). Greatness runs in your genes! Greatness is not about being better than someone else. Greatness is being the best version of yourself as you fulfill God's plan and purpose for your life.

BOUNDARY-DEFYING FAITH

Not many people remember October 14, 1947, when Air Force Captain Chuck Yeager set a record by flying an experimental rocket-powered plane faster than the speed of sound. Felix Baumgartner wasn't even born then, so hearing about such a feat couldn't have been the motivating factor for him to want to repeat it—but this time, without the airplane! Who does such things? What drives human beings to break the rules, stretch the boundaries, and open the gates of possibility for others to walk through?

Baumgartner was born in Salzburg, Austria, and still remembers that as a five-year-old boy he dreamed of flying through the sky, even drawing detailed pictures of it.[9] His childhood heroes were Neil Armstrong and Spider-Man. What Baumgartner dreamed about led him to join the Austrian army where he was a member of the parachute display team. Later he set a world record doing BASE jumps from buildings and bridges. He even strapped on a wing made of carbon fiber and soared across the English Channel. However, falling from 120,000 feet in freezing cold, dark space, and plunging at over seven hundred miles per hour to break the sound barrier would require Baumgartner to deal with a barrier he had not yet encountered: fear.[10]

Baumgartner and his team of over three hundred experts were constantly adjusting their strategy for success, overcoming as many unknowns as possible. There was the balloon that would lift him to the targeted height, the parachute that would deploy to carry him back to the ground, and the myriad things in between that were needed to help him survive.

One necessary piece of survival gear would also prove to be his nemesis—his space suit. The space suit was necessary to prevent him from freezing and to provide oxygen for breathing, among other things. Mirrors were attached to his gloves since his helmet prevented him from looking up to see if his parachute had deployed correctly. They even planned for a misting system inside his face mask in case his breath caused it to fog up.[11] But for Baumgartner, each time they added something to the suit, it also made it heavier and reduced his sense of control. Soon he began to have panic attacks when forced to spend hours testing inside this necessary encasing. The claustrophobia was too much. "Every skill I had developed over the years became pretty useless as soon as I stepped into the space suit. And after twenty-five years as a professional, it makes you feel weak and exposed."[12]

Six months after deciding to walk away from the project, Baumgartner was watching film footage of his replacement wearing his helmet with his name on it and doing his job in a test run. A twinge of envy overcame his anxiety, and he was compelled to return. When he did, he was faced with two additional things that would be equally difficult to overcome. First, his team had lost faith in his ability to follow through, so he would need to regain their confidence in him as a leader. Second, he would have to admit his weakness and seek professional help for the claustrophobia. Baumgartner was willing to do both.

Doubt and fear continued to plague him, but not the same as before. He had learned techniques to deal with his psychological issues. Now his greatest fear was failing to achieve his mission of supersonic flight. That fear ended when he fell to earth from a height of twenty-four miles on Sunday, October 14, 2012, at the top speed of 833.9 miles per hour, or Mach 1.24. He had done it! And about eight million people had watched it live.[13]

"It was harder than I expected," he said. "Trust me, when you stand up there on top of the world, you become so humble. It's not about breaking records any more. It's not about getting scientific data. It's all about coming home."[14]

Future pilots and astronauts will benefit from the data that was collected. New strategies for escape concepts and equipment solutions for loss of pressure will keep scientists and engineers busy for a long time to come. But Baumgartner learned a couple things that can help those whose motivation and drive will never come close to taking them to the stratosphere.

First, when Baumgartner stepped outside the module that carried him into space and looked out into the vastness, he said, "I know the whole world is watching, and I wish the whole world could see what I see. Sometimes you have to go up really high to understand how small you really are."[15] Faith takes you into new heights in God. Faith changes your perspective so that you are able to view your life from His perspective. Faith is breathtaking. It puts the awe back into your life.

Second, when a reporter asked afterward how he planned to beat that, he replied, "I don't have to. I reached a peak and I don't have to top it again. A lot of kids now think of me as Fearless Baumgartner—but I hope I can make fear cool. All these kids can know that Felix also has fear. So they can address their own fears."[16]

God may instruct you to do things that will cause you to fear. Faith says, "Do it anyway." One of the greatest weapons formed against the believer is fear, which travels with two other companions—anxiety and worry. These will stagnate your movement, growth, and development. Stop arguing with God when He shows you the things you can accomplish and the possibilities that lie ahead. Dare to step out of the shadows of others. Look fear in the face, and in faith determine to always do the greater thing!

Today I want you to declare, "I am moving into a new realm of faith in God. No more stagnation, no more limitations, no more fear. I progress and press past all limitation." Faith takes you into the realm of God. Whatever you do for God, you must do in faith.

> Hast thou faith? have it to thyself before God. [Shake the restriction off. Let God bring you out of psychological and emotional strongholds.] Happy is he that condemneth not himself in that thing which he alloweth. [When you take personal responsibility for your life, you either allow things or disallow it. Make certain you are happy with your decisions.] And he that doubteth is damned if he eat, because he eateth not of faith: for whatsoever is not of faith is sin.
>
> —ROMANS 14:22–23

It's one thing to have faith in God, but it is another thing to have faith in who God has made you to be. Most of us wish we were other people. We single out parts of ourselves that we don't like. Or worst still, we snuff out others who shine brighter than we do, trying to destroy their influence as well as other people's positive perception of them.

Have faith in who God made you to be. You are awesome. Stop putting yourself down. Stop belittling who you are. God did not make you flawed, but fabulous. After all, you were created in His image and His likeness.

Do not let others cheapen, depreciate, or devalue you—and never devalue yourself! Stop trying to fit in by lowering your standards and expectations. You are God's workmanship (Eph. 2:10). You are fearfully and wonderfully made (Ps. 139:14). Believe it, behave it, and become it.

You are not an accident, an incident, or a coincidence. Your life was created on purpose for a purpose. You are someone very special. God made you the way you are for a reason. You have heard this before, but it bears repeating: in this entire world, there is no one like you. Meditate on that before proceeding. Do you believe it? Can you conceptualize and embrace the fact that you are a one-of-a-kind treasure? You are here to give to the world your unique presence, perspective, gifts, abilities, and talents in the place you now live and the time you are here on earth. You are to shine as you display God's glory.

You have standout qualities that other people need to admire and desire, including your unique value and perspective in the marketplace and your execution of gifts and talents. You are the type of person other people should get to know. You have assets others would love to have, so put them on display. Your outlook, thoughts, and ideas, including your unique way of seeing things, really do make a difference. As you peer in the mirror, acknowledge that the special person you see is loved, celebrated, and wanted. You are worth more than anyone could ever compensate you for because of the unique blessing you bring to the world. But you must be faithful to protect and cultivate it.

Continually grow, courageously face challenges, and always give your best. By doing so, you help make this world a better place. And by the way, your best should never be compared to someone else's best. Your best is *your* best. The world needs you to develop *your* unique potential.

As you build your self-esteem and nurture your authentic self, never forget that not only are you immensely valuable but others are too. God created us all with unique perspectives and purposes. In celebrating yourself, don't forget to show gratitude for others, who, like you, also choose to give their best. Don't compete, don't get jealous, don't compare. Instead, celebrate yourself and others. Do the right things and God will honor you.

The people you celebrate may become the very people you need to collaborate with to maximize your own potential or partner with in fulfilling your dreams. You do well to surround yourself with passionate, purposeful, and persevering people who encourage and inspire you.

Have faith in God and His instructions for your life. Whatever He instructs you to do, believe that it is attached to a blessing and a good personal outcome.

After the jump, Baumgartner said, "The suit was my worst enemy, but it became my friend—because the higher you go, the more you need the suit. It gives you the only way to survive. I learned to love the suit up there. That's an even bigger message than flying supersonic."[17]

To suit up, "gird up the loins of your mind, be sober, and hope to the end for the grace that is to be brought unto you" (1 Pet. 1:13).

> Put on the whole armour of God, that ye may be able to stand against the wiles of the devil. For we wrestle not against flesh and blood, but against principalities, against powers, against the rulers of the darkness of this world, against spiritual wickedness in high places. Wherefore take unto you the whole armour of God, that ye may be able to withstand in the evil day, and having done all, to stand. Stand therefore, having your loins girt about with truth, and having on the breastplate of righteousness; and your feet shod with the preparation of the gospel of peace; above all, taking the shield of faith, wherewith ye shall be able to quench all the fiery darts of the wicked. And take the helmet of salvation, and the sword of the Spirit, which is the word of God.
>
> —Ephesians 6:11–17

You may have been seduced into believing that you are limited, that you have a glass ceiling that prevents you from a specific breakthrough because of your country of birth. Take heart today because there are no restrictions in the realm of the Spirit. Remember, Jesus was conceived in Nazareth, birthed in Bethlehem, protected in Egypt, then returned to Nazareth where He grew in wisdom, stature, and favor. He was baptized in the Jordan and tempted in the wilderness. Jesus began His ministry in Capernaum, performed His first miracle in Cana, and surrendered His will in Gethsemane. He was crucified on Golgotha, and His resurrection was substantiated on the road to Emmaus. When God is at work in your life and when purpose is known, no geographical boundaries can restrict God's work in, with, and through your life. Declare, "I have no geographic limitations."

Declare these over your life:

- My movement will be without the restrictions of fear, anxiety, or worry. By faith I decree that fear will place no limitations or lids upon me, for "God has not given us a spirit of fear, but of power and of love and of a sound mind" (2 Tim. 1:7, NKJV).

- I will accomplish that which God has commissioned and appointed me to do, achieve, invent, or innovate. I may have physical limitations, but I serve a God who is limitless. "With God nothing will be impossible" (Luke 1:37, NKJV).

- "Whatsoever things are true, whatsoever things are honest, whatsoever things are just, whatsoever things are pure, whatsoever things are lovely, whatsoever things are of good report; if there be any virtue, and if there be any praise, [I will] think on these things" (Phil. 4:8).

Living limitless does not infer that you are limitless but that the God you serve is limitless. "Have faith in God" (Mark 11:22). He will take you to new heights in your faith until you see things from His perspective. With men it is impossible, but "with God all things are possible" (Mark 10:27).

> For in him we live, and move, and have our being; as certain also of your own poets have said, For we are also His offspring.
>
> —ACTS 17:28

PART FOUR

· · ·

Restore

• • •

CHAPTER 10

Don't Complain; Create

The Law of Creativity

Let us make man in our image, after our likeness.
—Genesis 1:26

MAN WAS MADE in the image of God, but man was formed from the dirt of the earth. In one of the oldest books of the Bible a despairing man by the name of Job reminded God that He had fashioned Job from a lump of clay (Job 10:9). Though Job went through loss of children, property, and health, the final results of his life show that God knew what He was doing with that so-called lump of clay, even if Job had doubted it for a period of time. (See Job 42:12–17.) So it is with you and everyone else in this world. No one's life is so far gone that it cannot be reengineered.

HOPE MAKES THE IMPOSSIBLE POSSIBLE

Growing up in Pittsburgh, Bill Strickland watched his Manchester neighborhood go from trees and neat homes in the

1950s to a ghetto with the highest crime rate in the city in the 1960s. As a sixteen-year-old boy, he was almost flunking out of school and was looking for a way out. It's hard to believe that any young black man raised in poverty would consider art as a ticket to a better life, but that's exactly what happened.

One day Strickland was wandering down the hall of his high school and chanced to look inside a sunlit classroom and see a mound of clay on a potter's wheel being shaped into a pot. Strickland interrupted the teacher, Frank Ross; introduced himself; and asked to learn how to do ceramics.

The potter's wheel turning was like magic to him. "I saw a radiant and hopeful image of how the world ought to be. It opened up a portal for me that suggested that there might be a whole range of possibilities and experiences that I had not explored."[1]

The art teacher agreed to teach Strickland about ceramics—and much more. He told Strickland that he had "the talent and the resources to take control of his life and do something with it."[2] Having had no mentors or models of successful people before this, nor encouragement from others around him, it was a miracle that young Strickland chose to believe him. Ross invited Strickland into his home and poured food and encouragement into that young man when others saw nothing in him. He also introduced him to the music of the jazz greats—Miles Davis, Duke Ellington, John Coltrane, and others. Music, sunlight, art, and the smell of food cooking on the stove were all signs of hope.[3]

Strickland received a scholarship to the University of Pittsburgh, starting the year on probation and ending up on the dean's list. But his old neighborhood that he had come to care deeply about continued to suffer, as the riots of the late sixties plundered it. While still in college, Strickland decided to open an after-school program to bring hope back to the streets. He called it Manchester Craftsmen's Guild (MGC), and he taught the kids about pottery. It had changed his life, and he had every reason to believe that it would do the same for other kids as well.[4]

Three years later, he was asked to take over Bidwell Training Center, a church-run program that provided vocational training for adults. Accepting this challenge gave him his vision for saving troubled kids before they were lost and reclaiming adults who had been left behind by the system. By 1983 Strickland had amassed a network of business and community leaders whom he parlayed into the next grand adventure of social change. With $112 in the bank, Strickland set out walking the streets to raise $8 million to construct a building on an abandoned industrial park site.[5]

Strickland chose to build a place of beauty where sunlight poured in like it had in the classroom where he first saw Ross and his potter's wheel. "The worst thing about being poor is what it does to your spirit, not just your wallet. I wanted to build something that would give the people who come here a vision of what life could be, to create an environment that says that life is good."[6]

Three years later the building was completed. Today MCG educates hundreds of kids without charge in ceramics, painting, photography, and drawing. The goal is not to produce artists but to engage and redirect troubled young people and point them toward a better future. It must be working, because 80 percent of the kids who go through their doors go on to attend college.[7] As of 2016, Strickland's youth program has been "franchised" in ten other cities, including Akko Israel, "which serves Palestinian and Israeli kids together under one roof. Strickland hopes the Akko center will, in his words, 'possibly alter a conflict that has lasted for centuries.'"[8]

The adult training center has been equally successful. Strickland has partnered with area corporations to train a much-needed skilled workforce. These adults are being trained as technicians in the fields of horticultural technology, medical coding, and the culinary arts, among many others. Over five hundred adults graduate from the program each year, 90 percent of whom find full-time employment.[9]

Strickland still lives not far from his old neighborhood in a modest home. He has turned down numerous offers by Fortune 500 companies and even requests that he run for political office. Instead, he uses his time to do things like speak to young MBA students about how he is changing the world.[10] Business students like these, often with tears in their eyes, line up to ask how they can work for him, which still surprises him knowing they had originally set out in pursuit of high-paying corporate jobs. When he asks them about their original goal of one day becoming a high-profile CEO, they reply with an answer that sounds something like this: "We're here because we want to find an opportunity where life would make more sense. You make sense."[11]

Strickland's message is about "common sense and decency, about the dictate that our best hopes must always be acted upon, that all people everywhere possess an innate hunger for and right to the sustaining, the good, and the beautiful."[12] And his love of jazz? Well, Strickland included a state-of-the art jazz venue in his building, and since its inception, he has recorded some all-time jazz greats, winning MCG Grammys![13]

Strickland has both a sense of urgency to change the world, as well as a hope that it can be done. While introducing his model to a group of school kids in a new city where they were launching, a little girl raised her hand and asked how long it was going to take to be finished. When Strickland told her three to four years, she politely said, "Mr. Strickland, I don't have three or four years."[14] He shared that story with a group of businesspeople in that same city declaring:

> Poverty growing, neighborhoods dying — hope dying....Jobs are out there...People who want to work can't find them because they can't read, can't do basic math, and what's worse they can't imagine themselves reading or doing the math, much less working those good jobs to support their families. Something wrong with this picture.[15]

Strickland declares, "We can turn this whole story around to one of celebration and one of hope."[16]

Your country, city, and neighborhood are not without hope. Maybe that's why God planted you there. Esther was planted in Persia in a region where the king passed a decree to exterminate the Jewish people. But God's plan was greater than his. To manifest His plan on earth, He used a young woman from a rural village. She did not have a degree in political science.

149

She was not trained in constitutional law, hostage negotiation, or geopolitical conciliation and arbitration. But what she did have was faith in God.

I've discovered that God does not call the qualified, but He does qualify the called. The risks may be high, but the anticipated results and rewards far outweigh the risks. Ask God to use you to make a difference in your country, city, and neighborhood. Ask Him to show you, if necessary, how to create something out of nothing.

THE LAW OF CREATIVITY

God created. This we know from the first chapter of Genesis. And this is what this book you're holding in your hand is all about—creating the life of your dreams from what may seem like the formless, empty, dark void of your past. If you are still reading, you have come to understand that you have the agency—*and the God-given creativity*—to create whatever tomorrow you desire.

When God said in Genesis 1:26, "Let us make man in our image, after our likeness," He had a prototype in mind. Likewise, when you set out to create the life you've dreamed of, you must also keep in mind the likeness after which you want to create it. God gives us the kingdom of heaven as the prototype after which we are to fashion our lives.

The origins of the meaning of the word *create* are rooted in the Latin *creātus*, which is the past participle of *creāre*, which means "to bring into being, beget, give birth to, cause to grow."[17] If you look into the etymology of the word *create*, you will find that it is related to *crēscere*, meaning to "to come into existence, increase in size or numbers, grow."[18]

So what does this tell us about the law of creativity? I believe this speaks to the necessity of proactively making what we desire for ourselves and for our families grow. We must tend the gardens of our lives by cultivating and creating what we hope to see grow there. It is incumbent upon us to sow and till and plant whatever we want to produce—we are the stewards of the garden of our life.

Let me ask you: What are you growing in your day-to-day life? What are you creating?

To create is to grow—and to grow is to be a good and faithful steward. Meditate for a moment on the Parable of the Talents:

> The Kingdom of Heaven can be illustrated by the story of a man going on a long trip. He called together his servants and entrusted his money to them while he was gone. He gave five bags of silver to one, two bags of silver to another, and one bag of silver to the last—dividing it in proportion to their abilities. He then left on his trip.
>
> The servant who received the five bags of silver began to invest the money and earned five more. The servant with two bags of silver also went to work and earned two more. But the servant who received the one bag of silver dug a hole in the ground and hid the master's money.
>
> After a long time, their master returned from his trip and called them to give an account of how they had used his money. The servant to whom he had entrusted the five bags of silver came forward with five more and said,

"Master, you gave me five bags of silver to invest, and I have earned five more."

The master was full of praise. "Well done, my good and faithful servant. You have been faithful in handling this small amount, so now I will give you many more responsibilities. Let's celebrate together!"

The servant who had received the two bags of silver came forward and said, "Master, you gave me two bags of silver to invest, and I have earned two more."

The master said, "Well done, my good and faithful servant. You have been faithful in handling this small amount, so now I will give you many more responsibilities. Let's celebrate together!"

Then the servant with the one bag of silver came and said, "Master, I knew you were a harsh man, harvesting crops you didn't plant and gathering crops you didn't cultivate. I was afraid I would lose your money, so I hid it in the earth. Look, here is your money back."

But the master replied, "You wicked and lazy servant! If you knew I harvested crops I didn't plant and gathered crops I didn't cultivate, why didn't you deposit my money in the bank? At least I could have gotten some interest on it."

Then he ordered, "Take the money from this servant, and give it to the one with the ten bags of silver. To those who use well what they are given, even more will be given, and they will have an abundance. But from those who do nothing, even what little they have will be taken away. Now throw this useless servant into outer darkness, where there will be weeping and gnashing of teeth."

—Matthew 25:14–30, nlt

God has already given you whatever you need to produce, grow, and increase whatever He has entrusted you to do in this life. If you feel stuck, as perhaps Queen Esther did, then pray. Lean in and listen. He will give you the insight and inspiration you need to cultivate the beautiful thing He has put you in His garden to create—whether that be a conversation, a campaign, or a canvas you are to paint. Trust Him to enable you through His Spirit to do something new—to grow, produce, and increase whatever brings you joy. This is the law of creativity, as active and real as the law of gravity. And as does everything in the kingdom, it requires faith.

> If you keep quiet at a time like this, deliverance and relief for the Jews will arise from some other place, but you and your relatives will die. Who knows if perhaps you were made queen for just such a time as this?
> —ESTHER 4:14, NLT

◆ ◆ ◆

CHAPTER 11

Keep Hope Alive

The Law of Expectation

And God said, Behold, I have given you
every herb bearing seed, which is upon the
face of all the earth, and every tree, in the
which is the fruit of a tree yielding seed.
—Genesis 1:29

WHERE THERE IS a seed, there is hope. In every plant and
in the fruit of each tree, God provided a seed so it would
have a future. Everyone needs the hope of a good future in
order to move forward. The good news is that hope is in you
already, just as the seed is in the fruit. You never have to face
hopelessness because God is always at work in you. You can
expect good things!

HOPE SPRINGS ETERNAL

It could be said that hope is to faith what wet is to water. You
cannot have one without the other. While faith has to do with

trust, hope has to do with expectation. Hope and faith are like twins, each with distinguishing characteristics that you can learn to recognize. I would describe faith as having to do with something present though not yet seen, while hope is something that is not yet present but will be.

Hope fueled by faith is not the same as optimism. Pastor and author Henri Nouwen observes, "Optimism and hope are radically different attitudes. Optimism is the expectation that things...will get better. Hope is the trust that God will fulfill God's promises to us in a way that leads us to true freedom."[1] Hope, like faith, is a foundational Christian virtue that must be deliberately practiced. It is also, like faith, a spiritual force. Without the force of hope, human beings fade, and like flowers, they wilt. In Proverbs we read that without hope, the heart becomes sick (Prov. 13:12).

Hope is presumed to be something good that one desires and anticipates will happen in the future. To one, hope represents what is probable, but to another, it is more of a wish or a distant dream. Dallas Willard describes hope as "joyous anticipation of good"[2] Though it is not here yet or unseen, that hope is based on a promise that comes from God. Yet hope is not just a religious concept. Even atheists are hopeful because they hold a desire for a future they believe is possible.

Some point to the first signs of spring after a long winter as a description of hope. Spring has always come, and there is no reason to believe that in any given year spring won't again follow winter. In the depth of winter, you can picture yourself in the certain spring you know is on the way. You can see it with your mind's eye.

Hope is not a feeling, although feelings are supportive structures for hope. Hope is actually a cognitive process that is active, not passive. *Hoping* that you are going to get a new job but taking no action toward achieving that hope is simply wishful thinking. Yet people often understand hope as passive, effortless, painless, and sure. But hope is proactive, requiring effort, initiative, and self-sacrifice.

Hope is based on trust or confidence in a person or process, including yourself. If you don't trust enough in what you believe to act on it, then you are hopeless, not hopeful. When you activate your faith, hope is activated in the process. They support each other. Hope will increase your faith and vice versa.

People who have strong faith believe they can trust the promises of God, so they anticipate something in the future in accordance with their understanding of God's ways. But they still must act, and they will undoubtedly encounter struggle, discomfort, and change. Brennan Manning once wrote, "Hope knows that if great trials are avoided, great deeds remain undone, and the possibility of growth into greatness of soul is aborted."[3]

I encourage you to continue to discover the truth about faith and hope. As Galileo if often quoted as saying, "All truths are easy to understand once they are discovered; the point is to discover them."[4] Learn the truth about the power of hope and how to leverage that hope to undergird your faith.

TO HOPE OR NOT TO HOPE

Several years ago a group of four-year-olds became part of a study that has received plenty of commentary over the years—some agreeing with and others disputing the findings. It's hard to believe that marshmallows could be part of scientific research, but they were.

A researcher gave a preschooler a plate of marshmallows, then told the child he had to leave of the room. If the child waited until the researcher came back, she could have two marshmallows. But if she had to have one right away, she could ring a bell and the researcher would return right away. Some children waited so they could have two marshmallows, and many did not.[5]

In order to study *why* some children were able to wait, another group of researchers repeated the study years later, this time with a twist. The kids were first given some experiences in which they were promised something better—bigger crayons, for example—if they waited. The first group received the crayons as promised; the second group never received what was promised. In further tests those who had hoped but received nothing decided not to wait and ate the marshmallow. Those whose hope had been fulfilled chose to wait.[6]

Whether the marshmallow test proves anything or not may be debatable, but no one would deny that many people have had their hopes dashed. They no longer believe their future will be any better than their past. Hopelessness is a powerful roadblock in life. Perhaps you are familiar with the debilitating sense of hopelessness of those who are "without Christ, being aliens from the commonwealth of Israel, and strangers from the covenants of promise, having no hope, and without God in the world" (Eph. 2:12).

Hopelessness can be the result of unrealistic assumptions,

which can lead to blaming yourself for not being smart enough, fast enough, rich enough, or some other "enough." You *are* enough. Although you will never be perfect, you can be made perfect as you live in the bigness of God and His grace. He is able to perfect those things concerning you (1 Pet. 5:10).

That doesn't mean you stop growing, learning new skills, and finding new ways to achieve your preferred future. Failure is simply a process of discovery that may not have anything to do with your ability or your worthiness. Sometimes it is simply part of learning what is necessary for your ultimate success.

Hopelessness is often the result of believing you have no alternatives. Some would call that pessimism. But as nineteenth century French writer Alphonse Karr is quoted as saying, "We can complain because rose bushes have thorns, or rejoice because thorns have roses."[7] Rehearse God's promises: "For all the promises of God in Him are Yes, and in Him Amen, to the glory of God through us" (2 Cor. 1:20, NKJV). Manage the tension between your current situation and the promise for which you are believing.

Seemingly hopeless situations have led to tide-turning, history-making acts of courage, such as those of Johan van Hulst, who risked death by smuggling six hundred Jewish children out of Nazi-occupied Amsterdam.[8] He acted in spite of his hopeless situation, using hope as a catalyst to change the course of history. In other words, though the situation seemed hopeless, he was full of hope.

The same could be said of those brave men and women who on September 11, 2001, attempted to gain control of their hijacked plane before it became an instrument of destruction by terrorists. They lost their lives in a Pennsylvania field, but they saved the lives of countless others. When you feel hopeless, act anyway.

Here is a simple prayer to pray:

> *Heavenly Father, I come before You today in need of hope. There are times when I feel helpless to change things around me and to move on in life. Sometimes I feel too spiritually weak to pray. But today I pray for hope. I need hope to believe that things will get better. I need hope to have faith that things will turn around for my good. I need hope for a better future, a better marriage, better health, better work opportunities, better staff, better relationships, and a better mindset. I need hope for a better life. I need hope for love, joy, and favor.*

THE LAW OF EXPECTATION

This book is designed to bolster your faith, so I want you to understand how important it is to keep your expectation high. David said, "My soul, wait thou only upon God; for my expectation is from him" (Ps. 62:5). Faith and hope—trusting and expecting—work together.

Hopefulness is considered optimistic and a good thing, but in a longevity study researchers discovered that older people who are *overly* optimistic actually live fewer years. An article at Smithsonian.com reported that older people "who see only rainbows and sunshine ahead"—rather than acknowledging that death is a part of life—"are fooling themselves and are less likely to live healthy, cautious lives."[9] So being hopeful doesn't mean putting your analytical brain on snooze and acting as if everything will always work out perfectly. Assuming that hopefulness and ease are traveling partners can lead you to despair and pain when difficulties, setbacks, trials, failures, and even crises of faith come.

Paul wrote about Abraham's hope, saying he "against hope believed in hope, that he might become the father of many nations, according to that which was spoken" (Rom. 4:18). That hope fed Abraham's faith, and as a result "he staggered not at the promise of God through unbelief; but was strong in faith, giving glory to God; and being fully persuaded that, what [God] had promised, he was able also to perform" (vv. 20–21).

Paul himself was a man of persevering hope, but he found himself in several jail cells. Yet he observed, "Everything happening to me in this jail only serves to make Christ more accurately known, regardless of whether I live or die" (Phil. 1:20, msg).

Be open to growing in what you believe. Ask God to increase your hope so you can grow in faith. Do not be easily shaken in your mind when life throws you a curve ball. (See 2 Thessalonians 2:1–2.) When circumstances get tough, do not put your hope in things, people, ideas, or outcomes. If you do, you will end up disappointed for one reason or another. Put your hope in God.

> Why, my soul, are you downcast? Why so disturbed within me? Put your hope in God, for I will yet praise Him, my Savior and my God.
>
> —Psalm 42:5, niv

Encourage yourself by reflecting on a time when something new and unexpected came into your life. God is always with you. He will never give up, and neither should you.

I decree according to Job 11:16–19 that "you will surely forget your trouble, recalling it only as waters gone by" (NIV). Life will be brighter than noonday, and darkness will become like morning. You will be secure, because there is hope; you will look about you and take your rest in safety. You will lie down, with no one to make you afraid, and many will court your favor.

You may feel hopeless, but you are not helpless. Don't believe for one moment that your challenging circumstances have the power to diminish your happiness. Your happiness shouldn't be contingent on realizing a certain achievement, obtaining a certain goal, or marrying a certain person. If you feel sad, disappointed, or disheartened because something didn't happen or seems out of reach, then change the focus of your hope. No matter how good you thought it would be, nothing about your life journey should be considered as the proverbial season finale. God is all about new beginnings. His mercies are new every morning (Lam 3:22–23), so you can rewrite the script of any season with the dawn of each new day.

French philosopher Blaise Pascal wrote, "We are never living, but hoping to live; and whilst we are always preparing to be happy, it is certain, we never shall be so, if we aspire to no other happiness than what can be enjoyed in this life."[10] Stop wallowing, wailing, and waiting for things to change before you start to live! Jesus said, "The thief comes only to steal and kill and destroy; I have come that they may have life, and have it to the full" (John 10:10, NIV).

In this season, I decree that nothing and no one will steal your joy, suffocate your happiness, or stifle your progress in life. Stop putting your happiness on layaway for some distant time in the future. Play your happy music and dance now. Dance in the fire and sing in the lion's den, for this too shall pass.

By faith decree, "God, 'You turned my wailing into dancing; you removed my sackcloth and clothed me with joy, that my heart may sing your praises and not be silent. LORD my God, I will praise you forever!'" (Ps. 30:11–12, NIV). Worship God with reckless abandon. Decree with me at the top of your lungs, "Surely God is my help; the Lord is the one who sustains me.…I will sacrifice a freewill offering to you; I will praise your name, LORD, for it is good. You have delivered me from all my troubles, and my eyes have looked in triumph on my foes" (Ps. 54:4, 6–7, NIV).

Hope is connected to finding meaning in life. It is foundational to your happiness, success, and progress. God has great plans for you, and many awesome things await you in your future. That's not only something worth believing God for, it is worth hoping for.

> "For I know the plans I have for you," declares the LORD, "plans to prosper you and not to harm you, plans to give you hope and a future. Then you will call on me and come and pray to me, and I will listen to you. You will seek me and find me when you seek me with all your heart."
>
> —JEREMIAH 29:11–13, NIV

CHAPTER 12

— ◆ ◆ ◆ —

Live Your Awesome

THE LAW OF AMAZEMENT

And God saw every thing that he had
made, and, behold, it was very good.
—GENESIS 1:31

ON APRIL 10, 2019, the first image taken of a black hole was announced in a global press conference. The US National Science Foundation director, France Córdova, reflected the excitement at the success of the worldwide collaboration that led to this image by exclaiming, "We are seeing the unsee-able."[1] How prophetic! We are living in the days when we are seeing that which was previously unseen. Glory be to God! The ability to observe and understand what have until now been unobservable mysteries is just the beginning.

The outer edge of a black hole is called an "event horizon." That edge was revealed in the image captured by the scientists. I believe this is a prophetic metaphor for what is on the horizon for you, your family, your community, your industry, and your nation. In essence we are living in an extraordinary season of supernatural manifestation. That which is and always has been is now becoming seen as it manifests in our collective awareness on earth. Hallelujah! Glory be to God! I am inspired, because just as on April 10, 2019, a paradigm-shifting announcement was made about seeing the unseen, so I am declaring today that you will begin to see the supernatural manifest in your life.

> As it is written, Eye hath not seen, nor ear heard, neither have entered into the heart of man, the things which God hath prepared for them that love him. But God hath revealed them unto us by his Spirit: for the Spirit searcheth all things, yea, the deep things of God....Now we have received, not the spirit of the world, but the spirit which is of God; that we might know the things that are freely given to us of God. Which things also we speak...But the natural man receiveth not the things of the Spirit of God: for they are foolishness unto him: neither can he know them, because they are spiritually discerned.
>
> —1 Corinthians 2:9–14

Your new frontier lies just beyond your natural senses—not somewhere out in space, but in the unexplored regions of the kingdom within you. Your inner treasure deserves all the attention you can give it. You have potential yet to be maximized. It takes faith to see it, to believe it, to possess it, and to manifest it.

THE POWER IS IN YOU

As a believer, when you recognize the liberty Christ secured for you on the cross of Calvary, you should understand that you are not a prisoner of your past, a product of your environment, or a victim of circumstances. "It is for freedom that Christ has set us free. Stand firm, then, and do not let yourselves be burdened again by a yoke of slavery" (Gal. 5:1, NIV). You are not bound to the person you used to be because that no longer serves the person you have the power to become.

Your feelings and emotions are not who you are but are simply how you choose to respond to external stimuli. Your future doesn't have to take the same route as your past. Your destiny doesn't have to include your past relationships, experiences, and circumstances. You can sign a new lease on life, create a new paradigm, build new relationships, gain new skills and behaviors, and take advantage of new opportunities. You don't have to apologize to people for wanting something better. Stop asking people for their opinions when you can see how their opinions have undermined their own greatness!

You don't have to justify your feelings or actions when you are trying to figure out which way to go. Pray and consult with God, then trust Him despite the many people who say you are making a mistake. You don't have to put up with people who are insecure about your strengths, ideals, and Christian values. Some people want you to fail just to prove that Christianity is outdated. All you have to do is "walk by faith, not by sight" (2 Cor. 5:7), trusting that God knows what's best for you and that He will continue to lead you along the "paths of righteousness for His name's sake" (Ps. 23:3). With a positive outlook and an unshakable trust that God has a plan greater than the sorrow you left behind, nothing you set your mind to accomplish is beyond God's empowerment (Job 22:28).

I know from personal experience that when you change, not everyone will be pleased and celebrate the change. Some will be suspicious, some mildly irritated, while others will blatantly protest by giving you an ultimatum. But the people of quality—those who have been divinely assigned to you and those meant to be in your life as traveling companions—won't ask you to explain your change or justify the faith and courage you now have. They will see the sincerity of your heart and the beauty of a rejuvenated soul.[2] They already understand what it takes to put *awesome* back into a life, most likely because they had to traverse the same spiritual terrain as you. They will automatically identify with both your humanity and your spirituality when at one moment you reach the depths of hell and another you touch the sky, figuratively speaking.

Here is a story I believe will encourage you to put *awesome* back into your life. The story is told of an explorer. He recounts his experience traveling years ago in the Middle East.[3]

> When going down the Tigris and Euphrates rivers many years ago with a party of English travelers I found myself under the direction of an old Arab guide whom we hired up at Baghdad....He thought that it was not only his duty to guide us down those rivers, and do what he was paid for doing, but also to entertain us with stories curious and weird, ancient and modern, strange and familiar. Many of them I have forgotten, and I am glad I have, but there is one I shall never forget....

Said he, "I will tell you a story now which I reserve for my particular friends." When he emphasized the words "particular friends," I listened, and I have ever been glad I did....

The old guide told me that there once lived not far from the River Indus an ancient Persian by the name of Ali Hafed. He said that Ali Hafed owned a very large farm, that he had orchards, grain-fields, and gardens; that he had money at interest, and was a wealthy and contented man. He was contented because he was wealthy, and wealthy because he was contented. One day there visited that old Persian farmer one of those ancient Buddhist priests, one of the wise men of the East. He sat down by the fire and told the old farmer how this world of ours was made. He said that this world was once a mere bank of fog, and that the Almighty thrust His finger into this bank of fog, and began slowly to move His finger around, increasing the speed until at last He whirled this bank of fog into a solid ball of fire. Then it went rolling through the universe, burning its way through other banks of fog, and condensed the moisture without, until it fell in floods of rain upon its hot surface, and cooled the outward crust. Then the internal fires bursting outward through the crust threw up the mountains and hills, the valleys, the plains and prairies of this wonderful world of ours. If this internal molten mass came bursting out and cooled very quickly it became granite; less quickly copper, less quickly silver, less quickly gold, and, after gold, diamonds were made.

Said the old priest, "A diamond is a congealed drop of sunlight." Now that is literally scientifically true, that a diamond is an actual deposit of carbon from the sun.

The old priest told Ali Hafed that if he had one diamond the size of his thumb he could purchase the county, and if he had a mine of diamonds he could place his children upon thrones through the influence of their great wealth.

Ali Hafed heard all about diamonds, how much they were worth, and went to his bed that night a poor man. He had not lost anything, but he was poor because he was discontented, and discontented because he feared he was poor. He said, "I want a mine of diamonds," and he lay awake all night.

Early in the morning he sought out the priest...and when he shook that old priest awake out of his dreams, Ali Hafed said to him:

"Will you tell me where I find diamonds?"

"Diamonds! What do you want with diamonds?"

"Why, I wish to be immensely rich."

"Well, then, go along and find them. That is all you have to do; go and find them, and then you have them."

"But I don't know where to go."

"Well, if you will find a river that runs through white sands, between high mountains, in those white sands you will always find diamonds."

"I don't believe there is any such river."

"Oh yes, there are plenty of them. All you have to do is to go and find them, and then you have them."

Said Ali Hafed, "I will go."

So he sold his farm, collected his money, left his family in charge of a neighbor, and away he went in search of diamonds. He began his search, very properly to my mind, at the Mountains of the Moon. Afterward he came around into Palestine, then wandered on into Europe, and at last when his money was all spent and he was in rags, wretchedness, and poverty, he stood on the shore of that bay at Barcelona, in Spain, when a great tidal wave came rolling in between the pillars of Hercules, and the poor, afflicted, suffering, dying man could not resist the awful temptation to cast himself into that incoming tide, and he sank beneath its foaming crest, never to rise in this life again....

The man who purchased Ali Hafed's farm one day led his camel into the garden to drink, and as that camel put its nose into the shallow water of that garden brook, Ali Hafed's successor noticed a curious flash of light from the white sands of the stream. He pulled out a black stone having an eye of light reflecting all the hues of the rainbow. He took the pebble into the house and put it on the mantel which covers the central fires, and forgot all about it.

A few days later, this same old priest came in to visit Ali Hafed's successor, and the moment he opened that drawing-room door he saw that flash of light on the mantel, and he rushed up to it, and shouted:

"Here is a diamond! Has Ali Hafed returned?"

"Oh no, Ali Hafed has not returned, and that is not a diamond. That is nothing but a stone we found right out here in our own garden."

"But," said the priest, "I tell you I know a diamond when I see it. I know positively that is a diamond."

Then together they rushed out into that old garden and stirred up the white sands with their fingers, and lo! there came up other more beautiful and valuable gems then the first. "Thus," said the guide to me, and, friends, it is historically true, "was discovered the diamond-mine of Golconda, the most magnificent diamond-mine in all the history of mankind, excelling the Kimberly itself. The Kohinoor, and the Orloff of the crown jewels of England and Russia, the largest on earth, came from that mine."

When that old Arab guide told me the second chapter of his story, he then took off his Turkish cap and swung it around in the air to get my attention to the moral.... "Had Ali Hafed remained at home and dug in his own cellar, or underneath his own wheat fields, or in his own garden, instead of wretchedness, starvation, and death by suicide in a strange land, he would have had 'acres of diamonds.' For every acre of that old farm, yes, every shovelful, afterward revealed gems which since have decorated the crowns of monarchs."

When he had added the moral of his story, I saw why he reserved it for "his particular friends." But I did not tell him I could see it. It was that mean old Arab's way of going around a thing like a lawyer, to say indirectly what he did not dare say directly, that "in his private opinion there was a certain young man then traveling down the Tigris River that might better be at home in America."

Stop selling yourself short. You are a diamond in the rough. Upheavals deep beneath the surface of the earth push up magma that has diamonds in it. Diamonds go through heat and pressure to become the prized jewels that they are. The more you are tested and tried, the more light you will reflect. The more you overcome, the more valuable you become![4]

As *Robinson Crusoe* author Daniel Defoe once wrote, "The Soul is plac'd in the Body like a rough Diamond, and must be polish'd, or the Lustre of it will never appear."[5]

The word *diamond* originated from the Greek *adamas*, which translated means "invincible."[6] Being invincible includes the idea of not being conquerable. When we speak of individuals as being adamant, it means they are tough, resolute, immovable, unwavering, resolute, and unbending.

Life's upheavals bring your true hidden worth and value to the surface. From the places of hardship and pressure, from the broken places, your true worth, intelligence, gifts, and talents will emerge.

When people look at your life and what God has done for you, they can never imagine what it took to get you here. People admire your gifts, abilities, station, or status, but nobody knows what you went through, what you came up against, and which friends betrayed you along the way. They don't see the rejection, judgment, loneliness, falls, and failures you overcame. Nobody knows what you struggled with or how you smiled, danced, and raised your hands by faith. Nobody knows that faith was the catalyst that kept you going when giving up looked like a good option. Your faith in God and His promises got you through, especially this one from Romans 8:28: "We know that all things work together for good to those who love God, to those who are the called according to His purpose" (NKJV).

So many people are stuck in their past, hardened by the hardship or embittered by brokenness. But those of us who understand the process know that you are transformed by your trials. From them you arise from obscurity, emerging from the realm of the common into the realm of distinction. Like a diamond exquisitely set, your divine brilliance is put on display to the world by God Himself. Through years of intense heat and extreme pressure, the sooty beginning gives way to beauty, brilliance, and value. Enduring the heat and pressure, which transforms carbons into radiant carats, is a beautiful metaphor for the spiritual, mental, and emotional fortitude that is required for anyone to be transformed from ordinary to extraordinary.[7]

A DIVINE FORMULA

Life is like mathematics. According to 2 Peter 1:2–10, if you get the formulas right, you will always come out a winner! Consider the equations I've listed below, based on a text that was sent to me many years ago:

$2 + 4 = 6$

$5 + 1 = 6$

$6 - 0 = 6$

$6 + 0 = 6$

$8 - 2 = 6$

$7 - 1 = 6$

$10 - 4 = 6$

$14 - 8 = 6$

$12 \div 2 = 6$

$18 \div 3 = 6$

$60 \div 10 = 6$

$6 \times 1 = 6$

What is my point? My point is that even though the factors are different in each equation, each ends up with the same answer. So too God uses many variations to get you where He ultimately wants you to be. At times you add things and people into your life. At other times you must eliminate them. The time may come during which you need the multiplying effect of sowing seed, including how you invest your seeds of time, knowledge, and relationships. Later division and separation might be required. Not all of life's equations will be fun to solve. But the addition, subtraction, multiplication, or division is not as important as who you become in the process! Of course, obeying God's formula is always the best equation for you.

The process may differ from person to person, but the destination is always perfection in God. Trust Him that He knows what's best for you. Don't compare your life's equation to someone else's. The Lord may not take you through the same pathway He took your parents, friends, or colleagues. Each of our lives has different types of challenges. What matters is obeying Him so you arrive at your destination. What the devil meant for the worst, God can turn around for the best (Gen. 50:20; Deut. 23:5; Rom. 8:28). Don't give up on the process!

Here is God's mathematical formula for living a successful life:

Do you want more and more of God's kindness and peace? Then learn to know him better and better. For as you know him better, he will give you, through his great power, everything you need for living a truly good life: he even shares his own glory and his own goodness with us! And by that same mighty power he has given us all the other rich and wonderful blessings he promised; for instance, the promise to save us from the lust and rottenness all around us, and to give us his own character.

But to obtain these gifts, you need more than faith; you must also work hard to be good, and even that is not enough. For then you must learn to know God better and discover what He wants you to do. Next, learn to put aside your own desires so that you will become patient and godly, gladly letting God have his way with you. This will make possible the next step, which is for you to enjoy other people and to like them, and finally you will grow to love them deeply. The more you go on in this way, the more you will grow strong spiritually and become fruitful and useful to our Lord Jesus Christ. But anyone who fails to go after these additions to faith is blind indeed, or at least very shortsighted and has forgotten that God delivered him from the old life of sin so that now he can live a strong, good life for the Lord.

So, dear brothers, work hard to prove that you really are among those God has called and chosen, and then you will never stumble or fall away.

—2 PETER 1:2–10, TLB

Throughout this divinely ordained process, don't stop to cry or feel self-pity or regret. Don't stop at all. Keep moving on.

Don't look at your situation as if you have no hope. Remember, every circumstance contains within it the divine building blocks that God uses to build an awesome future for you and your loved ones.

You are the essential factor in the unfolding of God's plan. Do not reject the work of the Lord in your life. No matter what is added or subtracted, multiplied or divided by way of life experiences, you will always come out a winner. Your job is simply to add faith to all of life's equations, challenges, and problems! Believe in God. Believe in yourself and your ability to win through the One who has already won!

A FRACTION OF A DEGREE

Over time people discovered that precision cutting enhanced a diamond's brilliance. God is working in your life with the same precision to bring out your brilliance. As we have seen, the first chapter of Genesis walks us through a divine transformation process. This process happens over time, not all at once. "By little and little I will drive them out from before thee, until thou be increased, and inherit the land" (Exod. 23:30). If you daily make a small change that does not take much effort, by end of the year, you will have made 365 changes in your life!

Have you heard of the 1 percent rule? A little bit more effort seems to make all the difference. Just a one-degree change in temperature can transform hot water into steam, and with steam we can power a locomotive and generate electrical power to light up an entire city. In the Olympics in Beijing in 2008, Michael Phelps won the 100-meter butterfly swim by a hundredth of a second, winning his seventh gold medal.[8] The closest margin of victory at the Indy 500 in all the races since 1991 has only been .043 of a second.[9] A fraction of a second made all the difference.

I don't subscribe to the theory of evolution, but I find it interesting that evolutionary scientists say the genetic difference between a chimpanzee and a human is only 1.2 percent.[10] What a difference that 1 percent makes! Human beings have engineered ways to walk on the moon and live in space stations—something we surely can't say for chimpanzees. By making just a 1 percent change, you can create the future you want. You can determine your destiny.

THE LAW OF AMAZEMENT

Faith puts *amazing* back into your life. God called His creation "very good." Today we might say something like, "That is amazing!" Exercise your ability to marvel—to see the marvelous and to wonder in awe at the many amazing things taking place around you. Don't take the magnificence of life for granted. Don't neglect to look up at the sky on occasion in amazement—don't slumber through a beautiful sunrise or ignore a spectacular sunset because instead you're watching TV. You can choose to put awe, wonder, and amazement back into your life. This is what makes life rich. And it may also be what makes you rich. Think of all the bloggers and podcasters who have skyrocketed to celebrity status because they are able to see the amazing in what you or I dismiss as mundane.

Everything in your life is as you see it. In other words, as you've often heard said, "Beauty is in the eye of the beholder." Where one person bemoans their dated ceiling fan, another is delighting in having a ceiling! You can choose to wake up in the morning grumpy, or you can make a joyful noise to the Lord singing, "Oh What a Beautiful Mornin'" because you have eyes to see while others may be blind. You can choose to greet each day amazed at God's tender mercies, which are fresh and new every morning. And why are they so? Because He loves you afresh and new each day! He is amazed at the wonder and beauty of you.

God has made you a treasure to this world, but it takes hope-fueled faith to walk it out. You are God's gift to humanity, and how you live your life is your gift to Him. You owe it to both God and yourself to unearth your treasure of potential, earmarked for the generation into which you have been born. Let His glory shine brightly through you so the world may "see your good works, and glorify your Father which is in heaven" (Matt. 5:16). Let the world be amazed that through Him and because of Him you have focus in the midst of an array of distractions; you have peace in the midst of confusion; you are prospering in the midst of social, economic, and national uncertainty; you have abundance in the midst of lack; you have joy in the midst of challenges; you have strength over weakness; you have been blessed and progressed despite the insurmountable odds you had to overcome. You overcome temptation rather than being overcome by temptation; you choose good over evil and forgiveness over unforgiveness. These are just a few of the ways you can live an awesome life and demonstrate to others how awesome your God is.

Your success and prosperity have been secured in Christ, but you must choose to access it. It is one thing for you to pray, but are you willing to exert the energy it takes to discipline yourself and diligently pursue God's will? "Be ye doers of the word, and not hearers only, deceiving your own selves" (Jas. 1:22).

To get what you've never had, you must do what you have never done and go where you have never been. So push yourself. Your next push may be the one that advances you that fraction of a second that gets you to your dream. Everything you ever wanted lies just outside your comfort zone. Never be afraid to do something you have never done before.[11]

David had never fought a giant before Goliath. Esther had never delivered a people from ethnic cleansing before she had to confront Haman. Noah had never built a boat before the flood threated total annihilation. Peter had never walked on water before Jesus bid him to step out of the boat . Moses had never parted a sea until the Red Sea lay between his people and freedom.

Never underestimate the opportunity that lies within your crisis. The movie *Meet the Robinsons* ends with a quote from Walt Disney that says, "We keep moving forward, opening up new doors and doing new things, because we're curious...and curiosity keeps leading us down new paths."[12] These are paths of innovation, imaginations, success, and prosperity. God said in Isaiah 43:19: "Behold, I will do a new thing; now it shall spring forth; shall ye not know it? I will even make a way in the wilderness, and rivers in the desert."

Remember, the more life cuts away at us, like a diamond, the brighter we sparkle. As a diamond is masterfully chiseled to display the prismatic beauty of radiating light, so the master jeweler is cutting and chiseling away the superfluous so that you will reflect His light all the more brilliantly.

> You're here to be light, bringing out the God-colors in the world. God is not a secret to be kept. We're going public with this, as public as a city on a hill. If I make you light-bearers, you don't think I'm going to hide you under a bucket, do you? I'm putting you on a light stand. Now that I've put you there on a hilltop, on a light stand—shine! Keep open house; be generous with your lives. By opening up to others, you'll prompt people to open up with God, this generous Father in heaven.
>
> —MATTHEW 5:14–16, MSG

◆ ◆ ◆

Declarations

THROUGHOUT THIS BOOK you have learned about taking control of your thoughts, cultivating your greatness, preparing for your assignments, and speaking God's creative words in faith. Take a portion of these declarations each day and speak them out. "Faith comes by hearing, and hearing by the word of God" (Rom. 10:17, NKJV). Grow your faith by hearing your own mouth speak these words. Look up the scriptures and make them your own. Declare with confidence that God is for you and is cheering you on to success:

> Hear me, O LORD; for thy lovingkindness is good: turn unto me according to the multitude of thy tender mercies. And hide not thy face from thy servant…hear me speedily. Draw nigh unto my soul, and redeem it: deliver me because of mine enemies.
>
> —PSALM 69:16–18

I SPEAK OVER MY DAY

I arise today in total dependence upon You, decreeing and declaring the cancellation of all evil decrees over my year, my life, my family, my business, my possessions, my projects, my purpose, my neighborhood, my marriage, my community, my government, and my nation (Ps. 91:10).

Let every evil decree be replaced by Your original plans and purpose for my life now (Isa. 14:26–27).

I am hidden in You, God, dwelling in Your secret place and hidden under Your wings. I therefore decree I am not afraid of the arrows by day not the terror by night. You give angels charge over me to keep me in all of my ways (Ps. 91).

I decree that this day will be filled with strategic discernment and wise decisions (Prov. 12:5).

I decree this day I will be given access to supernatural might, strength, counsel, knowledge, and prophetic insight (Isa. 11:2).

I decree that every hour of this day is pregnant with promise and potential (Eccles. 3:1).

I speak light into every moment and insight into my most pressing needs, challenges, and problems. Only good can come out of them. Only good things and good gifts come to me from the Father of lights (Jas. 1:17).

Father, You are the God of creation and recreation. Please restore areas of my life that have been devastated, devalued, or destroyed (Joel 2:25).

Make beautiful every area that has been marred and bring alignment to every area that has been misaligned (Eccles. 3:11).

I speak peace into every hour of my day and declare they are filled with supernatural breakthroughs, extravagant favor, miraculous insight and foresight, and divine wisdom. No darkness, confusion, or fear will prevail against the peace of God that guards my heart and mind in Christ (Col. 3:15).

I decree and declare that every new day will bring a victory sweeter than the day before (Ps. 118:24–29).

I decree everything I set my heart and hands to will prosper (Deut. 16:15).

This day will be marked by a victorious, healthy, peace-filled, anxiety-free, grace-defined destiny (Phil. 1:6).

I declare that I will forever live under an open heaven and dwell in the supernatural favor of God (Deut. 11:13–15).

I arise today to take my rightful place above and not beneath, as the head and not the tail (Deut. 28:13).

I expect that You will grant me supernatural insight and strategies for how to work, organize my time, make decisions, and prosper in this assignment You have given me. Teach me to number my days, that I may apply my heart unto wisdom (Ps. 90:12).

Fill my mind with Your wisdom, understanding, knowledge, and the specific revelation of whatever it is I need to do to bring glory to Your name as I undertake every task and pass every test with Your infinite, manifest grace. I want to shine in the midst of darkness (Matt. 5:16).

I have been given all things pertaining to life and godliness— everything that I need to succeed today (2 Pet. 1:3).

Let wisdom guide my affairs. "For wisdom is better than rubies; and all the things that may be desired are not to be compared to it" (Prov. 8:11).

I choose to attack today with deliberate action based on vision, goals, and my personal dream for making this world a better place (Ps. 37:23).

I choose to live a life that is dynamic. I refuse to use alibis that begin with blaming others. I refuse to use others for selfish gain or as an alibi for the choices I make. I am the one who makes my decisions and therefore what does not work for me, I choose to discard. I choose to rely less on others and more on You. I choose to be patient with everyone as I expect the same from them (Prov. 3:31).

I decree:

- that I am free from fear and filled with faith
- that I am empowered to accomplish that which You have put me here to do
- that I will become all that I need to be in this season

Today I receive wisdom and new strategies for this new season I am in (Eccles. 3:1–2).

- I say goodbye to a poverty mindset.

- I say goodbye to poor decision making.

- I say goodbye to poor eating habits and inappropriate behaviors.

- I say goodbye to sickness and disease.

- I say goodbye to addictions.

I decree that:

- My mission is clear.

- My vision is unobstructed.

- My intentions are pure.

- My motivation is solid.

- My body, mind, soul, and spirit are healthy and strong.[1]

I DECLARE YOUR LOVE FOR ME

All things will work together for good for me because I love You (Rom. 8:28).

There is no good thing that You will withhold from me (Ps. 84:11).

I know You are for me and not against me (Rom. 8:31).

I know the thoughts You think about me are only good, and they are designed to give me hope and an amazing end (Jer. 29:11).

Let me never forget what Your Word says, that there is no fear in love and that perfect love casts out fear (1 John 4:17–18).

Your love for me is perfect. You love me just as I am, and You love me enough not to leave me as I am or forsake me (Deut. 31:6).

I want a new level of intimacy with You (Phil. 3:10).

I thank You for Your loving-kindness, which is better than life (Ps. 63:3).

I remind myself daily that your love never fails (1 Cor. 13:8).

I thank You for Your faithfulness even when I have been unfaithful to You (Deut. 7:9).

I reaffirm that You are my shepherd (Ps. 23:1).

I CHOOSE YOUR WILL

By Your Spirit I am empowered to let go when You remove things and people out of my life and to trust You in the process (Matt. 10:39).

Show me how to live a healthy life and to make the most effective and appropriate lifestyle changes that will yield healthy living (Gen. 1:26–31).

Show me how to avoid pitfalls and to overcome temptations (2 Pet 1:10–11).

Lead me along the paths of righteousness (Ps. 23:3).

Show me the path of life. "In thy presence is fulness of joy; at thy right hand there are pleasures for evermore" (Ps. 16:11).

- Show me how to live my best life.

- Show me practical steps for living a fruitful, faith-filled life.

- Show me how to be a better critical thinker.

- Empower me to move forward rather than looking back.

- Give me courage to walk away from things and people that are not good for me.

I am confident that You shall supply all of my need according to Your riches in glory (Phil. 4:19).

I have the mind of Christ, the Spirit of Christ, and the nature of Christ (1 Cor. 2:16).

I refuse to be conformed to this world, but I am transformed by the renewing of my mind (Rom. 12:1–2).

I am not a victim of circumstance.

- I choose focus over distraction.

- I choose peace over confusion.

- I choose life over death.

- I choose prosperity over poverty.

- I choose abundance over lack.

- I choose joy over sadness.

- I choose strength over weakness.

- I choose blessings over curses.

- I choose to overcome temptation rather than being overcome by temptation.

- I choose good over evil.

- I choose forgiveness over unforgiveness.

- I choose to attack every day with deliberate action based on my vision and goals.

Give me strength and clarity of mind so I can identify my purpose, maximize my potential, and follow the path You've mapped out for me (2 Pet. 1:1–10).

Help me to walk in Your light and live my life in the power and glory of Your kingdom (1 John 1:7).

I DECLARE THAT I TRUST YOU

I will be anxious for nothing (Phil. 4:6–7).

As I press toward the high calling of God in Christ Jesus, I am confident that the work You began in me will continue (Phil. 1:6; 3:14).

Let Your peace reign in my mind, in my family, at my place of work, in my business, and with my business partners (1 Sam. 25:6).

Let Your peace go before me when I go out and remain with me at all times (Isa. 55:12).

Give Your angels charge over me to watch over me while I am asleep (Ps. 91:11).

Give me Your wisdom and divine strategies to remove the stress from of my life (2 Cor. 13:11).

When I'm overwhelmed with the cares of life and can't seem to find my balance, be my Rock (Ps. 61:2).

I trust Your loving power and know that You will heal any stress, torment, and unrest. In my weakness Your strength is made perfect (2 Cor. 12:9).

I rest in the Lord and wait patiently for Him. I do not fret because of him who prospers in his way, because of the man who brings wicked devices to pass. I cease from anger and forsake wrath (Ps. 37:7–8).

MY DECLARATION OF INDEPENDENCE FROM YESTERDAY

"This moment is my defining moment, marking the ending of a sad...depressing...discouraging history, and the beginning of a prosperous, debt-free, disease-free, depression-free destiny"[2] (Deut. 28:1–14).

Today is the day I say goodbye to:

- self-defeating thoughts
- self-doubt
- self-deprecation
- bad attitudes
- bad habits
- self-defeating activities

- addictions
- staying in abusive relationships
- compromising my Christian values
- unproductive habits
- old ways of doing things that no longer work
- saying yes when I should say no
- allowing people to mistreat me
- mistreating others
- mediocrity and "good enough" activities
- unforgiveness
- resentment
- unhealthy competition
- fear
- doubt
- indifference
- hurt
- retaliation
- fears and phobias
- self-imposed prisons
- conforming to popular culture

- unhealthy soul ties

- toxic relationships and situations

- ineffective decisions or a poor decision-making process

- entertaining feelings of guilt

- thoughts that haunt late at night that say I'm not good enough

I decree I am delivered from:

- The people whom I made a priority, but they only made me an option.

- The game players and destiny-blockers.

- The dream assassins.

- The haunting memories of those who hurt me, disappointed me, and disrespected me.

- Those who didn't treat me with respect—I release them so that You can replace them with those who will treat me with respect.

- The ones who mistreated me, abused me, and didn't deserve to have me in their lives.

- Everyone who made my year harder, made my life miserable, and stood in the way of my success.

- The ones I allowed to hinder me from living the life You have planned for me.

- The ones who stopped me from dreaming and daring new things.

- The ones who laughed at my attempts to live for You, and to love and serve You, God.

- Weakness and areas of compromise, "for the good that I would I do not: but the evil which I would not, that I do. Now if I do that I would not, it is no more I that do it, but sin that dwelleth in me. I find then a law, that, when I would do good, evil is present with me" (Rom. 7:19–21).

- The resentment of every challenge I had to endure and the moments when the weakness of my flesh got the best of me. I look back with gratitude, knowing that in my weakness Your strength was made perfect. Most gladly therefore will I rather glory in my infirmities, that the power of Christ may rest upon me (2 Cor. 12:9).

- The inner turmoil and emotional pain that came with loving someone who didn't love me back.

- The hurt I felt from betrayal, abuse, misuse, and rejection.

- The pain of heartbreaks, breakups, and emotional breakdowns because now I know that every wrong relationship is bringing me one step closer to the right one.

- Staying when I should have left because I lacked the confidence to be alone with You. I now know that it is OK to be alone and that aloneness is not the same as loneliness. I also have learned that I don't have to stay in relationships where helping others is hurting me.

- Staying the same when I know I have to and can change for the best. I know staying means I am settling. Change means I'm not settling anymore. So I choose to go and grow and never to settle again.

- All my "*friend*emies" who betrayed me, lied to me, competed with me, undermined me, and gossiped about me. They served as an example of the people to avoid in the future.

- My bad eating habits and addictions that contributed to undermining optimal health. Give me a new lifestyle strategy. Thank You for giving me the grace to make the necessary adjustments, the discipline to embrace new habits and lifestyle decisions, and the will to live a healthy life. I am grateful to You for creating a healthy environment in which I live and the commitment to eat healthy and to exercise more. I refuse to be a couch potato.

- The ones to whom I gave my personal power when I became perturbed, disturbed, and depressed after discovering they laughed at my dreams. I decree the frustration I feel is now fuel that ignites my motivation and the catalyst of determination.

- Everything and everyone that weren't meant to be. I trust You in all things. You know who is and what is best for me.

- The words that hurt me and that play like a broken record in my head. I sever the attachments. I reject the words I couldn't shake off and the words that I thought defined me. I decree that by Your Word, by Your blood, and by Your Spirit that every soul tie and yoke is destroyed.

- Living a life of distraction, folly, immaturity and irresponsibility.

I decree that today is the day I am liberated from my past. This is my declaration of independence from my past, for whom the Son sets free is truly free indeed (John 8:36).

Help me not to repeat the mistakes of the past, but instead to learn from them (Prov. 8:12–21).

Help me to make better decisions (Ps. 25:4–5).

I decree I shall not establish new toxic relationships based on old relational strategies (1 Cor. 15:33–34).

I shall not complain about the past, but by faith I activate the new mercies commensurate to this new season, these new challenges, and this new day (Lam. 3:22–23).

Fill my mind with wisdom and the knowledge of my true identity (2 Cor. 5:17).

I decree that:

- I am empowered to accomplish that which I was born to do.

- I will become all that I was born to be.

- I am not an incident nor accident. There is no such thing as a coincidence.

- I use the freedom You have given me to make good decisions today that will affect the reality I will experience tomorrow.

- I recognize that You have created me as a free moral agent. I realize that my destiny is determined by my decisions.

I live forgiven. I forgive so that I may live without torment, regret, guilt, and grief. You said in Philippians 4:4–9: "Rejoice in the Lord always: and again I say, Rejoice. Let your moderation be known unto all men. The Lord is at hand. Be careful for nothing; but in every thing by prayer and supplication with thanksgiving let your requests be made known unto God. And the peace of God, which passeth all understanding, shall keep your hearts and minds through Christ Jesus. Finally, brethren, whatsoever things are true, whatsoever things are honest, whatsoever things are just, whatsoever things are pure, whatsoever things are lovely, whatsoever things are of good report; if there be any virtue, and if there be any praise, think on these things. Those things, which ye have both learned, and received, and heard, and seen in me, do: and the God of peace shall be with you."

I AM DELIVERED AND HEALED IN YOU

I decree that feelings of shame, fear and guilt will not overtake me, nor control me, but with Your help and empowerment, I will overcome by the blood of the Lamb and the word of my testimony (Isa. 54:4; Rev. 12:11).

I command fear, shame, and guilt to go in the name of Jesus (Rom. 8:1–2).

I know You have forgiven me, so today I forgive myself (1 John 2:12).

I close all opened doors that lead me away from You. Barricade those doors and take away Satan's access to my life (Gen. 4:7).

Build a hedge of protection around me (Job 1:10).

I repent of all rebellion and disobedience in my life and choose to live a life of obedience and consecration before You (2 Sam. 15:22).

I forgive those who hurt me (Matt. 6:14–15).

I bring all past hurt and trauma to You and ask that You heal me (1 Pet. 5:7).

I cancel past vows and all inappropriately spoken words, whether spoken by me or to me. "Set a watch, O LORD, before my mouth; keep the door of my lips. Incline not my heart to any evil thing, to practise wicked works with men that work iniquity" (Ps. 141:3–4).

I confess aloud that Jesus has borne every sin, hurt, and curse for me (Gal. 3:13).

I renounce cooperation with every spirit that has oppressed and controlled my life, including all addictions and carnality. I take back my personal power and assert my spiritual authority now (Luke 10:19).

I receive my deliverance and praise You, God, for Your unconditional love. I decree that I am delivered from every form of abuse.

- I am delivered from physical, psychological, verbal, emotional, and sexual abuse; financial or material deprivation; institutionalized abuse; and/or social oppression (intentional or unintentional exclusion from a valued activity, prejudice, denial of access to community events/groups, and/or being denied access to friends and family). I am delivered from discrimination ("oppressive and discriminatory attitudes toward a person's disability, including physical or learning disability, ill mental health, or sensory impairment; race, age, gender, religion, [and] cultural background"[3]).

- I assert that all people are equal and are endowed with inalienable rights that include life; liberty; access; and the pursuit of dreams, goals, vision, purpose, and potential.

Make my enemies to be at peace with me (Prov. 16:7).

Grant me peace of mind and calm my troubled heart (John 14:1).

When my emotions act like turbulent waters, speak peace to my soul (Ps. 55:18).

In my darkest hours, remind me that my breakthrough is on the way. I need Your light, Lord, in every way. Let the light of Your glory fill my soul (Ps. 119:105; 2 Cor. 4:6).

"The path of the just is as the shining light, that shineth more and more unto the perfect day. The way of the wicked is as darkness: they know not at what they stumble" (Prov. 4:18–19).

I have great peace because I love You, and nothing shall by any means hurt or harm me (Ps. 119:165).

I claim my peace that passes all human comprehension (Phil. 4:7).

When I am filled with anxiety, fear, and worry, remind me that You have not given me the spirit of fear but of power, love, and soundness of mind (2 Tim. 1:7).

I AM FREE IN CHRIST

The thief cannot steal, kill, or destroy. I have abundant life in Christ (John 10:10).

I am free indeed because Christ has set me free (John 8:36).

I am justified freely by His grace through redemption in Christ Jesus (Rom. 3:24).

I am under no condemnation because I am in Christ Jesus. I do not walk according to the flesh but according to the Spirit (Rom. 8:1).

In Christ Jesus I am free from sin and death (Rom. 8:2).

I am made alive in Christ (1 Cor. 15:22).

God has anointed and established me in Christ (2 Cor. 1:21).

God always leads me in triumph in Christ (2 Cor. 2:14).

I am a new creation in Christ; old things are gone, and everything has become new (2 Cor. 5:17).

I am a child of God through faith in Jesus (Gal. 3:26).

My past is past, and I kiss my past goodbye. God has removed my sin from me as far as the east is from the west (Ps. 103:12).

I forget those things that are behind and reach forward to my future, to the prize of my calling in Christ (Phil. 3:13).

I have been buried with Christ by baptism, so I will rise with Christ one day (Rom. 6:4).

In the future, when I feel paralyzed and trapped with no way out, I know from past experience that You will make a way (Isa. 51:10).

You will always help me to find my way out of sticky situations that threaten to undermine my purpose or my true identity in Christ (Ps. 91:3).

I may have pushed You away in the process of pushing others away. Forgive me for that (Ps. 73:28).

Make my enemies to be at peace with me (Prov. 16:7).

I declare that I will forever live under an open heaven. I stand fast in the liberty by which Christ has made me free, and I refuse to be entangled again with the yoke of bondage (Gal. 5:1).

Give Your angels charge over me to watch over me while I am asleep (Ps. 91:11).

Grant me peace of mind and calm my troubled heart (John 14:1).

Give me Your wisdom and divine strategies to remove the stress from of my life (2 Cor. 13:11).

When my emotions act like turbulent waters, speak peace to my soul (Ps. 55:18).

When I'm overwhelmed with the cares of life and I can't seem to find my balance, be my Rock (Ps. 61:2).

I trust Your loving power, and know that You will heal me of stress, torment, and unrest. In my weakness Your strength is made perfect (2 Cor. 13:9).

In my darkest hours, remind me that my breakthrough is on the way. I need Your light, Lord, in every way. Let the light of Your glory fill my soul (2 Cor. 4:6).

Help me to walk in the light of Your love and wisdom and live my life in the power and glory of Your kingdom (1 John 1:7).

I AM EMPOWERED IN YOU

I rely on Your power, which so greatly works within me (Col. 1:29).

Let Your priorities become mine, as You restore me with renewed energy (Ps. 119:37).

Let my work be energized by faith and my service motivated by love, hope, and unwavering faith in You (1 Thess. 1:3).

When I don't know what to do, Your Spirit will guide me (John 16:13).

I will wrestle with no one, for what already belongs to me. I need not compete with anyone. Instead of being deceived into believing someone wants to take my place, I will remember that my place cannot be taken (John 14:1–2).

I have no need to be disturbed or emotionally thrown out of kilter by those who attempt to undermine my purpose. I choose instead to perceive them as individuals who desire to do more and to be more even as I do myself, but who may lack the strategy to understand how to get what they want without fighting. I pray that they may find it.

I eliminate pride, arrogance, unhealthy competition, negativity, criticism, and cynicism by embracing my true identity (Col. 3:3–4).

I refuse to lose my identity, individuality, and authenticity by dumbing down or people-pleasing. I refuse to be a poor copy of someone else and assert my identity in Christ Jesus. I am fearfully and wonderfully made. I am a new creature in Christ Jesus (Ps. 139:14–17; 2 Cor. 5:17).

With Your help I will reach my fullest potential in You (Eph. 1:5,11).

You have not given me the spirit of fear, but of power, love and soundness of mind. I therefore cannot and will not give up or give in to any emotions I feel right now (2 Tim. 1:7).

I am not easily shaken in my mind (2 Thess. 2:2).

Grant me out of the riches of Your glory to be strengthened and spiritually energized with power through Your Spirit indwelling my innermost being and personality (Eph. 3:16)

I am more than a conqueror in Christ (Rom. 8:37).

No weapon formed against me shall prosper as I abide under the shadow of Your wings (Isa. 54:17).

"The adversaries of the LORD shall be broken to pieces; out of heaven shall he thunder upon them: the LORD shall judge the ends of the earth; and he shall give strength unto his king, and exalt the horn of his anointed." I decree my horn is exalted (1 Sam. 2:10).

By faith, I will succeed by attracting to myself the virtues, forces, and resources I wish to use, and I will invite the cooperation of other people who work with me to do the same (Heb.11:1-6).

I change my attitude toward life and mindset about my life so that it is in alignment with Philippians 4:8: "Whatsoever things are true, whatsoever things are honest, whatsoever things are just, whatsoever things are pure, whatsoever things are lovely, whatsoever things are of good report; if there be any virtue, and if there be any praise, think on these things."

I choose:

- blessings, not curses (Deut. 30:19).

- life, not death, "the thief cometh not, but for to steal, and to kill, and to destroy: I am come that they might have life, and that they might have it more abundantly" (John 10:10).

- abundance, not scarcity. Let the eyes of my understanding be enlightened; that I may know what is the hope of my calling, and what the riches of the glory of Your inheritance in the saints, and what is the exceeding greatness of Your power to us-ward who believe, according to the working of his mighty power (Eph. 1:18–19).

- success over failure. I realize that successful people are just getting started when failure has given up (Prov. 24:16).

- focus over distractions (Prov. 31:25–27).

"Blessed be the God and Father of our Lord Jesus Christ, who hath blessed [me] with all spiritual blessings in heavenly places in Christ: according as he hath chosen [me] in him before the foundation of the world, that [I] should be holy and without blame before him in love: having predestinated [me] unto the adoption of children by Jesus Christ to himself, according to the good pleasure of his will, to the praise of the glory of his grace, wherein he hath made [me] accepted in the beloved. In whom [I] have redemption through his blood, the forgiveness of sins, according to the riches of his grace; wherein he hath abounded toward [me] in all wisdom and prudence; Having made known unto [me] the mystery of his will, according to his good pleasure which he hath purposed in himself" (Eph. 1:3–9).

I decree Deuteronomy 28:1–14 over my life:

> And it shall come to pass, if thou shalt hearken diligently unto the voice of the LORD thy God, to observe and to do all his commandments which I command thee this day, that the LORD thy God will set thee on high above all nations of the earth: and all these blessings shall come on thee, and overtake thee, if thou shalt hearken unto the voice of the LORD thy God. Blessed shalt thou be in the city, and blessed shalt thou be in the field. Blessed shall be the fruit of thy body, and

the fruit of thy ground, and the fruit of thy cattle, the increase of thy kine, and the flocks of thy sheep. Blessed shall be thy basket and thy store. Blessed shalt thou be when thou comest in, and blessed shalt thou be when thou goest out. The LORD shall cause thine enemies that rise up against thee to be smitten before thy face: they shall come out against thee one way, and flee before thee seven ways. The LORD shall command the blessing upon thee in thy storehouses, and in all that thou settest thine hand unto; and he shall bless thee in the land which the LORD thy God giveth thee. The LORD shall establish thee an holy people unto himself, as he hath sworn unto thee, if thou shalt keep the commandments of the LORD thy God, and walk in his ways. And all people of the earth shall see that thou art called by the name of the LORD; and they shall be afraid of thee. And the LORD shall make thee plenteous in goods, in the fruit of thy body, and in the fruit of thy cattle, and in the fruit of thy ground, in the land which the LORD sware unto thy fathers to give thee. The LORD shall open unto thee his good treasure, the heaven to give the rain unto thy land in his season, and to bless all the work of thine hand: and thou shalt lend unto many nations, and thou shalt not borrow. And the LORD shall make thee the head, and not the tail; and thou shalt be above only, and thou shalt not be beneath; if that thou hearken unto the commandments of the LORD thy God, which I command thee this day, to observe and to do them: and thou shalt not go aside from any of the words which I command thee this day."

I will make declarations and undertake initiatives that are in alignment with my vision, goals, and purpose (Job 22:28).

I have clearly written down a description of my definite purpose, aim, and mission in life, and I will never stop until I shall have developed sufficient skills, gifts, abilities, talents, resources, networks, sponsorships, relationships, partnerships, opportunities, training, development, and confidence in whom and whose I am, all that I was meant to be, to do, to achieve and to accomplish the life of my dreams (Hab. 2:2–3).

I choose to lead and not follow because I am the head and not the tail, I am first and not last, and I am above only and not beneath (Deut. 28:13).

Father, when I succeed, I will give You thanks. If I fail, fall, or falter, I will at once arise again with new strength. I will learn from my mistakes and missteps and seek the grace of God for an alternative strategy (Eph. 5:20).

I DECLARE MY WORSHIP FOR YOU

I declare:

> "I will mention the lovingkindnesses of the LORD, and the praises of the LORD, according to all that the LORD hath bestowed on us, and the great goodness toward the house of Israel, which he hath bestowed on them according to his mercies, and according to the multitude of his lovingkindnesses" (Isa. 63:7).

"Now unto him that is able to do exceeding abundantly above all that we ask or think, according to the power that worketh in us, unto him be glory in the church by Christ Jesus throughout all ages, world without end" (Eph. 3:20–21).

Amen.

NOTES

— ♦ ♦ ♦ —

INTRODUCTION

1. Robyn Castellani "Want to Change Your Life? Change
   Your Narrative. Here's How," *Forbes*, July 17, 2018, https://
   www.forbes.com/sites/break-the-future/2018/07/17/
   want-to-change-your-life-change-your-narrative-heres-
   how/#6632c3781a9f.
2. Castellani, "Want to Change Your Life?"
3. Kelly McGonigal, *The Upside of Stress* (New York: Avery,
   2015), 27.
4. Read *Hello, Tomorrow!* to learn more.

CHAPTER 1: PUT FIRST THINGS FIRST

1. Fritz Chery, "Atheism," Bible Reasons, June 23, 2018,
   https://biblereasons.com/atheism.
2. Chery, "Atheism."
3. Blue Letter Bible, s.v. "*re'shiyth*," accessed September 19,
   2019, https://www.blueletterbible.org/lang/lexicon/lexicon
   .cfm?Strongs=H7225&t=KJV.
4. See *Commanding Your Morning* to learn more.
5. Arnold Bennett, *How to Live on Twenty-Four Hours a Day*
   (New York: George H. Doran Co., 1910), 27–28.
6. Blue Letter Bible, s.v. "*bara*," accessed September 19,
   2019, https://www.blueletterbible.org/lang/lexicon/lexicon
   .cfm?Strongs=H1254&t=KJV.
7. See *Reclaim Your Soul* to learn how.
8. See *The Prosperous Soul* to learn more.
9. Read *Hello, Tomorrow!* to learn how you can craft a vision
   for your life.

10. Enroll in Kingdom School of Ministry at kingdomu.net.

CHAPTER 2: START WHERE YOU ARE

1. Michael Jacob, "Genesis and Genealogy," Word of God International Ministries, accessed October 22, 2019, http://www.wogim.org/gengeo.htm.
2. Robert Greene, *The Laws of Human Nature* (New York: Viking, 2018), 72–75.
3. Greene, *The Laws of Human Nature*, 74–75.
4. Viktor E. Frankl, *Man's Search for Meaning*, trans. Ilse Lasch (Boston: Beacon Press, 2017), 111.
5. For more on these topics, refer to my best sellers *Commanding Your Morning* and *Hello, Tomorrow!*
6. Caroline Leaf, "How Prayer Affects the Brain," Dr. Leaf, June 1, 2015, https://web.archive.org/web/20151013034705/http://drleaf.com/blog/how-prayer-affects-the-brain/.
7. Caroline Leaf, *Switch on Your Brain* (Grand Rapids, MI: Baker Books, 2013), 28.
8. Leaf, "How Prayer Affects the Brain."
9. See *Reclaim Your Soul* to learn how to break free from emotional soul ties.
10. Paraphrased from *American Dictionary of the English Language, Webster's Dictionary 1828*, s.v. "blessed," accessed October 22, 2019, http://webstersdictionary1828.com/Dictionary/blessed and *Merriam-Webster*, s.v. "blessed," accessed October 22, 2019, https://www.merriam-webster.com/dictionary/blessed.
11. Blue Letter Bible, s.v. "*Ziklag*," accessed October 22, 2019, https://www.blueletterbible.org/lang/Lexicon/Lexicon.cfm?strongs=H6860&t=KJV.

12. Matt Schudel, "H. Wayne Huizenga, Florida Billionaire and Sports Franchise Owner, Dies at 80," *Washington Post*, March 23, 2018, https://www.washingtonpost.com/local/obituaries/h-wayne-huizenga-florida-billionaire-and-sports-franchise-owner-dies-at-80/2018/03/23/813dfafc-2eae-11e8-8ad6-fbc50284fce8_story.html.

13. Steven Almond, "Citizen Wayne—The Unauthorized Biography," *Miami New Times* 9, no. 33 (December 1–7, 1994), http://www.corporations.org/wmi/huizenga.html.

CHAPTER 3: SEPARATE, SEPARATE, SEPARATE

1. Online Etymology Dictionary, s.v. "discern," accessed October 22, 2019, https://www.etymonline.com/word/discern#etymonline_v_11382.

2. For more on this topic, read *The 40 Day Soul Fast*.

3. Blue Letter Bible, s.v. "*hagiazō*," accessed October 22, 2019, https://www.blueletterbible.org/lang/lexicon/lexicon.cfm?Strongs=G37&t=KJV.

4. Henry Morris, "Dividing Light From Darkness," *Days of Praise*, Institute for Creation Research, March 9, 2008, https://www.icr.org/article/dividing-light-from-darkness/.

5. Cindy Trimm, *Hello, Tomorrow!* (Lake Mary, FL: Charisma House, 2018), 114.

CHAPTER 4: BRING ORDER TO YOUR LIFE

1. Mike Vance and Diane Deacon, *Think Out of the Box* (Franklin Lakes, NJ: Career Press, 1995), 58, https://www.amazon.com/Think-Out-Box-Mike-Vance/dp/1564141861.

2. Tom Harris, "How Whales Work," HowStuffWorks, accessed October 22, 2019, https://animals.howstuffworks.com/mammals/whale.htm.

3. Rick Warren, *The Purpose Driven Life* (Grand Rapids, MI: Zondervan, 2003), 228.

CHAPTER 5: CHOOSE POTENTIAL OVER PROBLEMS

1. Winston Churchill, *Churchill: The Power of Words*, ed. Martin Gilbert (Boston: Da Capo Press, 2012), 7–8.
2. Shiza Shahid, "'Malala Is a Miracle': A Friend's Tribute to Clinton Global Citizen Award Recipient Malala Yousafzai," HuffPost, updated November 27, 2013, https://www.huffpost.com/entry/malala-is-a-miracle-a-tri_b_4005636.
3. Enroll in Kingdom Economics and Biblical Finance for an in-depth study of the seed.
4. Oxford Dictionaries, s.v. "potential," accessed October 22, 2019, https://en.oxforddictionaries.com/definition/potential.
5. This quote is often attributed to Winston Churchill, but its origins are unknown. See Richard M. Langworth, *Winston Churchill, Myth and Reality: What He Actually Did and Said* (Jefferson, NC: McFarland & Company, Inc. Publishers, 2017), 216.

CHAPTER 6: UNDERSTAND THE POWER OF TIME

1. Variations of this quote are circulating on the internet. A similar quote is attributed to Marc Levy, "Marc Lévy Coffret 2 Volumes Quotes," Good Reads, accessed October 15, 2019, https://www.goodreads.com/quotes/969007-if-you-want-to-know-the-value-of-one-year.
2. John Bradshaw, *The Letters of Philip Dormer Stanhope, Earl of Chesterfield, With the Characters* (London: Swan Sonnenschein & Co., 1892), 302.

3. *Merriam–Webster*, s.v. "undivided," accessed October 15, 2019, https://www.merriam-webster.com/dictionary/undivided.

4. E. M. Bounds, *Purpose in Prayer* (New York: Fleming H. Revell Company, 1920), 21.

5. Visit www.endyouryearstrong.com to learn more.

6. Read *Hello Tomorrow!* to learn how.

7. Visit www.trimmcoaching.com to learn more.

CHAPTER 7: EMBRACING THE POWER OF YOUR ASSIGNMENT

1. Russell H. Conwell, "The History of Fifty-Seven Cents," sermon, December 1, 1912, https://library.temple.edu/pages/46.

2. Blue Letter Bible, s.v. "*pro*," accessed October 23, 2019, https://www.blueletterbible.org/lang/lexicon/lexicon.cfm?strongs=G4253&t=KJV.

3. Blue Letter Bible, s.v. "*horizō*," accessed October 23, 2019, https://www.blueletterbible.org/lang/lexicon/lexicon.cfm?strongs=G3724&t=KJV.

4. Blue Letter Bible, s.v. "*proorizō*," accessed October 23, 2019, https://www.blueletterbible.org/lang/lexicon/lexicon.cfm?Strongs=G4309&t=KJV.

5. Blue Letter Bible, s.v. "*palah*," accessed October 23, 2019, https://www.blueletterbible.org/lang/lexicon/lexicon.cfm?Strongs=H6395&t=KJV.

6. Blue Letter Bible, s.v. "*pala'*," accessed October 23, 2019, https://www.blueletterbible.org/lang/lexicon/lexicon.cfm?Strongs=H6381&t=KJV.

7. Joel F. Drinkard Jr., "Number Systems and Number Symbolism," *Holman Illustrated Bible Dictionary*, ed. Chad Brand (Nashville: B & H Publishing Group, 2015), 1169.

8. Tim Sharp, "2019 Moon Phases Calendar," April 10, 2019, https://www.space.com/18880-moon-phases.html.

9. *Speech of the Right Hon. B. Disraeli, M.P., at the Banquet of the National Union of Conservative and Constitutional Associations at the Crystal Palace*, on Monday, June 24, 1872 (London: R. J. Mitchell and Sons, 1872), 11.

10. Kare Anderson, "Who Packs Your Parachute?," *Forbes*, November 18, 2015, https://www.forbes.com/sites/kareanderson/2015/11/18/who-packs-your-parachute/#67a75249717d.

11. Amy Morin, *13 Things Mentally Strong People Don't Do* (New York: Harper Collins, 2014).

12. Morin, *13 Things Mentally Strong People Don't Do*, vii–viii.

13. Morin, *13 Things Mentally Strong People Don't Do*, 9.

14. Morin, *13 Things Mentally Strong People Don't Do*.

15. "Marie Curie the Scientist," Marie Curie, accessed October 23, 2019, https://www.mariecurie.org.uk/who/our-history/marie-curie-the-scientist.

CHAPTER 8: PRACTICE THE ART OF ABUNDANCE

1. Daniel Lapin, *Thou Shall Prosper: Ten Commandments for Making Money* (Hoboken, NJ: John Wiley & Sons Inc., 2002), 150.

2. Lapin, *Thou Shall Prosper*, 150.

3. Visit www.trimmfoundation.org to learn more.

4. "The Multiplier Effect of Local Independent Businesses," American Independent Business Alliance, accessed October 23, 2019, https://www.amiba.net/resources/multiplier-effect/.

5. Fareed Zakaria and Lee Kuan Yew, "Culture Is Destiny: A Conversation With Lee Kuan Yew," *Foreign Affairs* 73, no. 2 (1994): 113–114.

CHAPTER 9: DEVELOP A DOMINION MINDSET

1. Steve Hartman, "The Other Team's View of the Ohio Miracle Game," CBS Interactive Inc., November 7, 2014, https://www.cbsnews.com/news/the-other-team/.

2. Hartman, "The Other Team's View of the Ohio Miracle Game."

3. Hartman, "The Other Team's View of the Ohio Miracle Game."

4. Paul Daugherty, "Facing Death, Lauren Hill Teaches Us Life Lessons," *USA Today*, October 26, 2014, https://www.usatoday.com/story/sports/ncaaw/2014/10/26/womens-basketball-lauren-hill-cancer-life-lessons/17959745/.

5. Hartman, "The Other Team's View of the Ohio Miracle Game."

6. Hartman, "The Other Team's View of the Ohio Miracle Game."

7. Abby Philip, "Lauren Hill, Who Was Determined to Play College Basketball Despite Cancer, Dies At 19," *Washington Post*, April 10, 2015, https://www.washingtonpost.com/news/early-lead/wp/2015/04/10/former-mount-st-josephs-basketball-player-lauren-hill-dies-of-brain-cancer-at-19/?noredirect=on.

8. Blue Letter Bible, s.v. *"Tso`ar,"* accessed October 23, 2019, https://www.blueletterbible.org/lang/lexicon/lexicon.cfm?Strongs=H6820&t=NKJV.

9. Donald McRae, "Felix Baumgartner: 'I Hope I Can Make Fear Cool,'" *The Guardian*, November 2, 2012, https://www.theguardian.com/sport/2012/nov/03/felix-baumgartner-space-jump-interview.

10. Tim Lamont, "Skydiving From the Edge of Space: Can a Human Break the Sound Barrier?," *The Guardian*, September 4, 2010, https://www.theguardian.com/

science/2010/sep/05/felix-baumgartner-michel-fournier-supersonic.

11. Lamont, "Skydiving From the Edge of Space."

12. McRae, "Felix Baumgartner."

13. John Tierney, "24 Miles, 4 Minutes and 834 M.P.H., All in One Jump," October 14, 2012, https://www.nytimes.com/2012/10/15/us/felix-baumgartner-skydiving.html.

14. Tierney, "24 Miles, 4 Minutes and 834 M.P.H., All in One Jump."

15. Tierney, "24 Miles, 4 Minutes and 834 M.P.H., All in One Jump."

16. McRae, "Felix Baumgartner."

17. McRae, "Felix Baumgartner."

CHAPTER 10: DON'T COMPLAIN, CREATE

1. Sara Terry, "Genius at Work," Fast Company, August 31, 1998, https://www.fastcompany.com/34692/genius-work.

2. Terry, "Genius at Work."

3. John Brant, "What One Man Can Do," Manuseto Ventures, September 1, 2005, https://www.inc.com/magazine/20050901/bill-strickland.html.

4. Terry, "Genius at Work."

5. Terry, "Genius at Work."

6. Terry, "Genius at Work."

7. Brant, "What One Man Can Do."

8. Kevin Kearns et al., "Bill Strickland and the Manchester Bidwell Corporation," Johnson Institute for Responsible Leadership, Fall 2016, http://www.johnsoninstitute-gspia.org/Portals/25/PDFs/Bill_Strickland.pdf?ver=2016-12-21-131152-743.

9. Brant, "What One Man Can Do."

10. Brant, "What One Man Can Do."

11. Terry, "Genius at Work."
12. Brant, "What One Man Can Do."
13. Terry, "Genius at Work."
14. Brant, "What One Man Can Do."
15. Brant, "What One Man Can Do."
16. "Bill Strickland: Rebuilding a Neighborhood With Beauty, Dignity, Hope," TED Conferences LLC, February 2002, https://www.ted.com/talks/bill_strickland_makes_change_with_a_slide_show?language=en#t-2069821.
17. *Merriam-Webster*, s.v. "create," accessed October 23, 2019, https://www.merriam-webster.com/dictionary/create.
18. *Merriam-Webster*, s.v. "create."

CHAPTER 11: KEEP HOPE ALIVE

1. "Living With Hope," Henri Nouwen Society, January 16, 2019, https://henrinouwen.org/meditation/living-with-hope/.
2. Dallas Willard, "Willard Words," Dallas Willard Ministries, accessed October 24, 2019, http://old.dwillard.org/resources/WillardWords.asp.
3. Brennan Manning, *Abba's Child: The Cry of the Heart for Intimate Belonging* (Colorado Springs, CO: NavPress, 2015), 87.
4. "Galileo Galilei Quotes," Goodreads, accessed October 23, 2019, https://www.goodreads.com/quotes/64597-all-truths-are-easy-to-understand-once-they-are-discovered.
5. Jacoba Urist, "What the Marshmallow Test Really Teaches About Self-Control," *The Atlantic*, September 24, 2014, https://www.theatlantic.com/health/archive/2014/09/what-the-marshmallow-test-really-teaches-about-self-control/380673/.

6. James Clear, "40 Years of Stanford Research Found That People With This One Quality Are More Likely to Succeed," James Clear, accessed October 22, 2019, https://jamesclear.com/delayed-gratification.

7. "Alphonse Karr Quotes," Goodreads.com, accessed October 23, 2019, https://www.goodreads.com/quotes/67318-we-can-complain-because-rose-bushes-have-thorns-or-rejoice.

8. Richard Sandomir, "Johan van Hulst, Who Helped Save 600 Children From the Nazis, Dies at 107," *New York Times*, April 1, 2018, https://www.nytimes.com/2018/04/01/obituaries/johan-van-hulst-who-helped-save-600-children-from-the-nazis-dies-at-107.html.

9. Rose Eveleth, "Pessimists Live Longer Than Optimists," Smithsonian.com, February 28, 2013, https://www.smithsonianmag.com/smart-news/pessimists-live-longer-than-optimists-525.

10. As quoted in John Eldredge, *Desire* (Nashville: Thomas Nelson, 2007), 104.

CHAPTER 12: LIVE YOUR AWESOME

1. "Astronomers Capture First Image of a Black Hole," National Science Foundation, April 10, 2019, https://www.nsf.gov/news/news_summ.jsp?cntn_id=298276.

2. For a guide to rejuvenating your soul, see *The 40 Day Soul Fast*.

3. Russell Herman Conwell and Robert Shackleton, *Acres of Diamonds* (New York: Harper & Brothers Publishers, 1915), 3–9.

4. See my book *Prevail* for more on this topic.

5. James T. Boulton ed., *Selected Writings of Daniel Dafoe* (London: Cambridge University Press, 1975), 32.

6. David Bressan, "The Origin of Geological Terms: Diamonds," *Forbes*, April 30, 2016, https://www.forbes.com/sites/davidbressan/2016/04/30/the-origin-of-geological-terms-diamonds/#93e4e52ae456.

7. For more on this topic, read my book *Prevail*.

8. "Michael Phelps Wins 7th Gold Title by a Finger Tip," Olympic.org, accessed October 23, 2019, https://www.olympic.org/videos/michael-phelps-wins-7th-gold-title-by-a-finger-tip.

9. "Driver Records & Milestones," IMS LLC, accessed October 23, 2019, https://www.indianapolismotorspeedway.com/events/indy500/history/driver-records-milestones/race-milestones.

10. "Genetics," Smithsonian National Museum of Natural History, accessed October 23, 2019, https://humanorigins.si.edu/evidence/genetics.

11. For more on this, read my book *PUSH*.

12. Josh Salvation, "Meet the Robinsons Ending HD," YouTube, July 25, 2016, https://www.youtube.com/watch?v=AoXD6Y7CXMU.

APPENDIX

1. "Decrees and Declarations for a New and Fruitful Day," City of Faith Prayer Boot Camp, August 1, 2017, http://prayerbootcamp.blogspot.com/2017/08/decrees-and-declarations-for-new-and.html.

2. "Decrees and Declarations for a New and Fruitful Day," City of Faith Prayer Boot Camp.

3. Cindy Trimm, *Rules of Engagement* (Lake Mary, FL: Charisma House, 2008), 66.

I am so happy you read my book.

I hope this book has helped you move beyond the self-defeating behaviors and mind-sets of the past and embrace the "awesome" person God designed you to be!

As my way of saying *thank you*, I'm offering you a gift.
- **E-book download:** *Hello, Tomorrow!*

To get this **FREE GIFT**, please go to
CINDYTRIMMBOOKS.COM/FREEGIFT

THANKS AGAIN, AND GOD BLESS YOU,

Cindy Trimm

CHARISMA
HOUSE